30259
29.95
Last activity never

HANDS-ON SCIENCE

for the

ACTIVE LEARNING CLASSROOM

Phil Parratore

SkyLight

Training and Publishing Inc.

The Curriculum Center
SAU Box 1389
Magnolia, AR   71753-5000

Hands-On Science for the Active Learning Classroom

Published by SkyLight Training and Publishing Inc.
2626 S. Clearbrook Dr., Arlington Heights, IL 60005
Phone 800-348-4474, 847-290-6600
Fax 847-290-6609
info@iriskylight.com
http://www.iriskylight.com

Creative Director: Robin Fogarty
Managing Editor: Ela Aktay
Acquisitions Editor: Regina Ward
Editor: Sue Schumer
Book Designer: Bruce Leckie
Cover and Illustration Designer: David Stockman
Indexer: Schroeder Indexing
Production Supervisor: Bob Crump

The activities in this book should be performed according to the instructions and safety notes provided. The publisher and author accept no responsibility for any damage caused or sustained while performing the activities in this book.

LCCCN 97-62544
ISBN 1-57517-079-5

2178-2-98V
Item Number 1591

06 05 04 03 02 01 00 99 98   15 14 13 12 11 10 9 8 7 6 5 4 3 2 1

Dedicated to my father,
whose love of science
was my inspiration.

CONTENTS

SECTION THREE

Balloons, Bubbles, and Toys

SECTION FOUR

Hot and Cold Stuff

SECTION FIVE

In Living Color

SECTION SIX

Static in the Attic

SECTION SEVEN

Air and Water Pressure

SkyLight Training and Publishing Inc.

INTRODUCTION

Do you find yourself looking for new ideas to get your students motivated about your science lessons? If teachers want to get their students really excited about scientific concepts, the activities employed need to be simple, quick to understand, and inexpensive to perform. In addition, they need to have a high "WOW" factor. Hands-on science activities that students encounter in your class or that you recommend for doing at home make great material for your parent newsletters. Such communications and the activities themselves allow parents to interact with their children about what they are learning, helping them contribute something positive and rewarding toward their children's science education.

Most of the activities in *Hands-On Science for the Active Learning Classroom* are effective at the primary and intermediate elementary levels and can easily be adapted to the secondary level. In my 27 years as a devoted "hands-on" math and science instructor at the middle school level, I have performed numerous science shows and demonstrations before thousands of kindergarten through sixth grade students. They love seeing (and doing) the demonstrations as much as my seventh and eighth grade students. In addition, I have taught and trained hundreds of teachers on the art of simple hands-on science experimentation. For secondary-level students, sometimes the demonstration of a simple experiment drives home a complex concept encountered in advanced science courses.

Beginning hands-on science teachers can start with the simple experiments first. Try them at home, and pick and choose the experiments that fit your students' needs. You will be amazed at their positive reactions. One reason that evaluating principals respond positively to a hands-on instructional approach is that many of them are familiar with how multiple intelligences are tapped holistically through such instruction. (For a brief description of the theory of multiples intelligences, you may refer to the chart on page 197 in the blacklines section.)

Hands-on learning is active learning. The positive research in support of active learning is overwhelming. The hands-on approach operates at many levels in a challenging classroom. Active learning gives students a chance to do something that produces immediate results during your science lesson. By the use of the activities in this book, you can plan science lessons that engage a student's thinking processes in learning and applying scientific knowledge. The new national science standards and benchmarks detail the use of active learning in today's science classrooms, but, to me, a key component of active learning is that it is fun. Yes, pure fun! Observe how your students interact during the active learning process. Observe the smiles on their faces and the sparkle in their eyes. Oh, by the way, you can enjoy the process and have fun, too.

HOW TO USE THIS BOOK

Hands-On Science for the Active Learning Classroom contains 90 exciting, fun, and easy-to-do experiments or activities that can immediately be implemented into your daily science lessons. Each activity has the following elements:

❑ **Purpose**, which states the scientific objective or goal of the activity.
❑ **When to Use**, a feature offering three pieces of key information for the teacher:
  • **Level** or ranking in terms of difficulty of the activity, ranging from 1 (easy) to 4 (more complex).
  • **Curricular Area**, an indication as to the specific discipline of science and area of study to which the activity applies.
  • **Time**, an estimation of how long it takes to complete the activity.

SkyLight Training and Publishing Inc.

- ❏ **What You Need**, which lists all the materials necessary for performing the experiment, including equipment and quantities. Most materials used can be found around the home or at your local supermarket, crafts store, hardware store, or drugstore.
- ❏ **What to Do**, which lists a step-by-step approach to exactly how an activity should be performed. Do not skip or substitute steps. When a special warning is in order for a particular activity, a Safety Note will be included in this section of the active. This note will highlight any precautions about potential hazards. Of course, caution should always be used when household chemicals and heating sources are part of an activity. Activities suitable only for teacher demonstration will be identified as such in the Safety Note.
- ❏ **Explanation**, which briefly discusses what happens in the experiment and how the results relate to the Purpose or objective of the activity.
- ❏ **Variation**, a feature offered for selected activities for which a different version or versions of a particular experiment are suggested.

As student reflection is a very crucial component of the scientific inquiry method, a "Student Reflection" page is included in the blacklines section at the back of this book. Students can use this simple form for each activity in order to get a deeper understanding of the scientific concepts being covered.

In addition, you may want to integrate a mathematics and statistics unit with your science lesson by having students take the result of their own individual experiments, plus those performed by several other classmates, and have them chart the results using one or more different types of graphs (for instance, a line, pie, or bar graph). Once again, the act of recording and organizing data has multiple benefits that address the visual/spatial, logical/mathematical, and naturalist intelligences; the meeting of goals, standards, and benchmarks; and the facilitating of students' transfer of learning into their lives by further processing the lesson.

When doing any experiments or activities in this book, it is recommended that you first read the complete activity and

carefully follow all instructions and safety precautions. As a further note of caution for any of the experiments in this book, if you are asking your students to try substitutions, it is recommended that they be directed to seek your approval first so that no potentially hazardous situations arise.

Deepening Science Experiences Through Block Scheduling

When it comes to interactive science experiments and activities, it always seems teachers and students never have enough time to really "dig" into an activity in depth. Recently adapted or under consideration in many school districts, a "block schedule" or "block time" allows the teacher to take several periods of class time and combine them together to form one long class period or block. This allows the teacher and students more quality time to work on specific activities without interruption.

If you have never used "block time" before, it is quite simple. Arrange your lesson plans so you have at least one hour or more of uninterrupted classroom time to work on the "hands-on" activities. In schools that don't already have block scheduling, arrangements can sometimes be developed cooperatively between the principal and teaching staff. As a teacher participating in block scheduling, you are not really cutting out time from other subjects because all these activities can become an integrated part of the regular core academic subjects of mathematics, social studies, and language arts.

The following are some additional suggestions for you to consider in terms of the activities in this book and the use of a block schedule.

❑ Break students into small groups of two or three and allow students to choose one or two activities from those that relate to your present curriculum. You may have students reflect in writing on how these activities relate to scientific concepts they are studying.

❑ Integrate activities into your math, social studies, and language arts units by having students write, calculate, and research additional information about the objective or "Purpose" section of these activities.

❑ Allow students to write their own hands-on science experiments and, with your approval, allow them time to perform the experiments in class. Consider videotaping the performances as part of your professional portfolio assessment.

❑ Have your students play "teacher" by having them write letters to their own parents or guardians about what they are doing with their various scientific activities. They should include a complete description of the scientific concepts being explored in class.

❑ Invite your students to choose several of their favorite activities and adapt them for younger students (either students in lower grades or younger siblings at home). Make arrangements for your students, with approval, to give the adapted activities to their younger counterparts to experiment with on their own.

❑ Have students convert the measurement of materials from one system to another, such as from the English system to the metric system (ounces to grams, inches to centimeters, and so on). For example, for a given experiment students can record results using the first system and then repeat the activity after converting the measurement of materials to the other system, comparing results accordingly. In addition, students can change the amount of one or more of the materials, so that a material can then be treated as a variable (see section on variables and constants below). This data can then be collected and charted or graphed as part of an integrated mathematics or statistics unit.

❑ Let students search the World Wide Web on the Internet for information related to a particular experiment. Have them locate a favorite search engine such as WebCrawler, Yahoo, Lycos, Infoseek, Image Surfer, or Alta/Vista. Students can type in one or two keywords from a favorite experiment (such as those referred to in the Procedure or the Curricular Area section) and surf the net. You and your students may be surprised at the amount of material available.

❑ Have students select a topic and continue their research using an encyclopedia, in printed form or CD-ROM version.

❑ Organize students in cooperative groups and have them analyze certain activities they have performed, discussing the scientific concepts being demonstrated and their implications for society and the environment. Keep this activity very open-ended so thoughts and ideas can flow freely.

The Variable and Constants

Have your students identify the variable and the constants in each activity. Remind your students that the factor being tested in an experiment is called the *variable.* In any experiment, only one variable is tested at a time. Otherwise, it would not be clear which variable caused the result of the experiment. *Constants* are factors that stay exactly the same in an experiment, never changing. Let's look at a couple of the experiments in terms of the variable and constants .

In Activity 7 (Magic Smoke Rings) the dry ice is the variable whereas the water and the food coloring are two of your constants. What actually causes the smoke is the presence of the dry ice. To prove this, do the activity as stated, except in Step 4 substitute some other material for the dry ice, such as an ice cube or a piece of frozen food. You will observe that no smoke rings are produced.

In a more complex experiment, Activity 63 (A Crystal Garden), students will find that the combination of the salt, ammonia, and bluing (the variables) is necessary for this experiment to work—that is, for crystallization to occur. The charcoal, food coloring, pie pan, water, and mixing bowl are constants. If you change one of the variables, the experiment will not work. Substitute vinegar for ammonia, for instance, and observe the result.

THE SCIENCE JOURNAL

As students identify constants and variables and make observations during their experimentations, they can list those variables and constants and write their observation notes in a science journal. You may ask students to include the Student Reflection sheet, included in the blackline masters section of this book, in their journals. When students are writing about the "what" and the "how" of each science activity, they will be employing higher-level thinking skills. This will encourage creative thinking and, at the same time, promote the scientific method, which is discussed in the following section.

THE SCIENTIFIC METHOD

An integral part of the science experience is becoming familiar with the scientific method. This is the universal, systematic testing of ideas,

SkyLight Training and Publishing Inc.

predictions, inferences, and hypotheses, a method originally developed by Galileo. To apply the scientific method, students may make notes in their science journals as they perform experiments, following the six steps listed on the next page.

1. State the PURPOSE or what you are testing in question format.
2. Form a HYPOTHESIS, an educated guess of what you expect to happen as a result of your testing.
3. Develop a PROCEDURE to test your hypothesis. This should be a detailed step-by-step listing of exactly how the experiment is run.
4. Gather DATA and observations.
5. Record RESULT(S). These are the specific observations and measured outcomes of the experiment.
6. Form CONCLUSION. This is the interpretation of your results. Your experiment either proves or disproves your hypothesis or is inconclusive and may lead to further retesting of the hypothesis.

In the real world of scientific research, it is this further experimentation that leads to scientific breakthroughs.

BEYOND THE CLASSROOM

Many educators know from experience that student learning is extended and reinforced when the outside, the real world, is brought to the classroom or when students explore that outside world themselves. In this section are some suggested activities that will provide opportunities for learning about science that go beyond regular classroom instruction.

Have students perform some of their favorite experiments or hands-on activities before their classmates or other students. Encourage your students to practice certain experiments at home first, with friends or family members being their audiences.

Set up booths in the classroom where students can perform selected science experiments and exhibit models to demonstrate various scientific concepts. Invite other classes or school visitors, in general, to visit the booths.

On a larger scale, organize a school science fair with your class. Invite colleagues, parents, your principal, and school board members to be judges. Ask your local newspaper to cover the story. Integrate art in the process by having students design invitations and posters to advertise the science fair. And do not forget to videotape the event.

Contact local industrial businesses and environmental groups, inviting to your classroom a spokesperson—such as an engineer, technician, or scientist—to discuss how science affects daily life in the community. Many companies and organizations welcome opportunities to get involved with school and community affairs. Your local chamber of commerce may assist you with finding such business to contact.

Since real-world science applications and career education are such important components of a well-rounded education, consider arranging a field trip for your class to tour a local factory, scientific institution, or public utility plant or office. An option is to arrange personal meetings for selected students to interview plant managers, research scientists, engineers, maintenance, or office staff from such companies. Students may then write their interviews for publication in a class newsletter or the school newspaper, or they may speak about their experiences before the class or even before a school assembly.

Another activity you may use in connection with career education is to write a job description for a career in a scientific field, posting the opening on a "HELP WANTED" bulletin board in class. Then have your students conduct mock job interviews, taking turns playing the role of the employer and the prospective employee.

Invite students' parents, grandparents, or other community members who are in science-related professions (such as physicists, optometrists, doctors, nurses, engineers, technicians, and industrial research or environmental scientists) to be guest speakers. Ask these professionals to share with your class information on the role of science in terms of their careers, allowing time for a question-and-answer session afterwards. Encourage your students to prepare questions for the guest speaker beforehand.

PERFORMANCE ASSESSMENT

Authentic assessment of hands-on science includes evaluation of conceptual understanding, performance evaluation of hands-on experi-

     SkyLight Training and Publishing Inc.

ences, application of knowledge, and communication of learning. You and your students can assess skills by using such methods as paper-and-pencil tests, laboratory/practical exams, self- and peer-evaluations, learning logs, journals, conferencing, student observations, and observation checklists.

An effective, proven evaluation tool that is readily accepted by students, parents, and administrators is the rubric. A rubric is a rule or guideline that outlines the criteria and indicators of success, often being used for evaluation and scoring purposes. The indicators in a rubric are observable, measurable behaviors that show to what degree a student is using his or her knowledge and skills.

A performance rubric for knowledge and skills provides a way for the science teacher, or any teacher, to evaluate student progress in terms of a particular unit or learning goal. A scoring rubric designed for the hands-on science teacher is offered in the blacklines section at the back of this book. You may wish to adapt the objectives or criteria in this rubric to fit the curriculum as well as the needs and ages of your students.

When using a rubric, a numerical ranking is often used for each objective, employing a sliding scale such as 1 (lowest) to 4 (highest). If you use each of the 16 objectives in the rubric on page 199, the maximum score would be 64 (16 objectives multiplied by the maximum ranking of 4). In my own teaching practice, I then assign a percentage for the entire performance assessment and that is the final grade a student receives. So if a student scores a 53 out of 64, her percentage/score would be 53/64—that is, 82.8%. This percentage can be then transferred into a standard grading system, such as 90% = A, 80% = B, 70% = C, and so on. Of course, you may use the rubric at your discretion and adapt your grading method and procedures to your individual school situation.

A FINAL WORD

I strongly encourage you to use this book to enhance your students' active learning process as well as a catalyst to develop your own science experiments and project ideas. Active learning works in the science classroom because it is student-centered, hands-on learning. As students experience the freedom to gather scientific data and organize it themselves, they also experience the excitement and pure raw power of being capable, competent learners. As your students self-evaluate, they experience the joy of giving themselves credit for a job well done and realize that any product (or performance) can be improved. Active learning works because it empowers students and encourages them to want to learn more.

SECTION ONE

WILD AND CRAZY REACTIONS

Have you ever seen rust form on a car or on a metal fence? Not long before, these objects glistened in the sun. But something happened that gave them a reddish-brown color and flaky appearance. Rusting (or oxidation) is just one of many kinds of chemical changes that go on around us every day. A hamburger being cooked on a grill, flowers growing and blooming, calories burned up in the human body or, likewise, gasoline burned in a car's engine are all actions during which properties change. These changes are essentially chemical reactions. In the activities in this section, you and your students will take a fun look at how certain actions cause chemical reactions in everyday life.

BOUNCING POPCORN

 ACTIVITY-AT-A-GLANCE

Purpose

Shows a chemical reaction involving common household products.

When to Use

Curricular Area	Difficulty Level	Time to Do
Acids and Bases	2	**5 minutes**

What You'll Need

- ❏ Water
- ❏ Clear glass or cup
- ❏ Vinegar
- ❏ Baking soda
- ❏ Toothpicks
- ❏ Unpopped popcorn
- ❏ Spoon

What to Do

1. Fill up the cup with water and then add 2 ounces of vinegar.
2. Add a pinch of baking soda and stir.
3. Add a few kernels of the popcorn.
4. Add a few more pinches of the baking soda.
5. Using a toothpick, poke at the bubbles forming around the popcorn. Then observe the popcorn kernels as they sink.

Explanations

The chemical reaction between baking soda and vinegar produces a gas called carbon dioxide. Carbon dioxide is an invisible gas, but in this experiment you can actually see the carbon dioxide in the form of bubbles. These bubbles, which are lighter than the water/vinegar solution, attach themselves to the popcorn kernels and float to the top of the cup. When the bubbles hit the air, they burst and the kernels drop back into the cup.

CHALK IT UP

 ACTIVITY-AT-A-GLANCE

Purpose

Simulates the effect of acid rain on buildings.

When to Use

Curricular Area	Difficulty Level	Time to Do

Acid Rain; Chemical Change

1 minute

What You'll Need

- ❏ 2 clear glasses or cups
- ❏ 2 pieces of chalk
- ❏ Vinegar
- ❏ Water

What to Do

1. Fill one glass ³/₄ full of vinegar.
2. Fill the other glass ³/₄ full of water.
3. Place a piece of chalk in each glass.
4. Observe and note the differences in reaction.

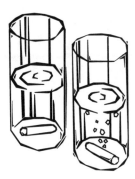

Explanation

The chalk starts to bubble in the vinegar while producing a gas. The chalk in the water does not bubble. Vinegar is acetic acid, while chalk simulates a mineral called limestone. Limestone was and still is used in the construction of many buildings. Access acid in our environment, in the form of acid rain, will eat away at limestone over many years in much the same way the vinegar eats away at the chalk.

Variation

Even though the reaction takes place immediately, keep the chalk in the vinegar overnight, and then observe what happens. Also, try squirting lemon or grapefruit juice (citric acids) onto a piece of chalk and observe the bubbly reaction.

DON'T HOLD YOUR BREATH

 ACTIVITY-AT-A-GLANCE

Purpose

Demonstrates the presence of carbon dioxide in exhaled breath.

When to Use

Curricular Area	Difficulty Level	Time to Do
Health; Chemical Changes		

5 minutes
(plus overnight settling time)

What You'll Need

Part A:
- ❏ Pickling lime (food canning section of grocery store)
- ❏ 2 quart clear glass jars, with lids
- ❏ Water
- ❏ Tablespoon

Part B:
- ❏ Straw
- ❏ Clear cup or glass

SkyLight Training and Publishing Inc.

What to Do

Part A: Making Limewater

1. Fill one of the jars about ²/₃ full of water.
2. Add 1 tablespoon of the pickling lime and stir.
3. Cap the jar and allow it to stand, undisturbed, overnight.
4. The next day, pour off the clear liquid into the second jar. The clear liquid in the second jar is called limewater.
5. Be careful not to pour any of the settled powder into the second jar.

Part B: Testing Your Breath

1. Pour a few ounces of the limewater into the glass.
2. Place the straw at the bottom of the glass and slowly exhale into the limewater. Keep blowing into the straw until the liquid changes colors.

 SAFETY NOTE: Caution students not to inhale on the straw and not to taste or drink the limewater. Although it isn't poisonous, the taste of limewater is unpleasant.

Explanation

The liquid turns from clear to a milky white solution called limewater, which is a compound that consists of water and calcium atoms. Limewater is a chemical indicator, which detects the presence of carbon dioxide gas. A chemical reaction occurs when carbon dioxide molecules (carbon dioxide being the gas we exhale after each breath) mix with the limewater.

VOLCANIC ACTION

ACTIVITY-AT-A-GLANCE

Purpose

Simulates a volcanic eruption by use of a chemical reaction.

When to Use

Curricular Area	Difficulty Level	Time to Do

Earth Formations; Chemical Changes

2

10 minutes

What You'll Need

- ❏ Baking soda
- ❏ Spoon
- ❏ Empty plastic soda bottle, any size
- ❏ Glass baking pan

- ❏ Dry dirt
- ❏ 1 cup of vinegar
- ❏ Red food coloring
- ❏ Funnel
- ❏ Topsoil

SkyLight Training and Publishing Inc.

What to Do

1. Place 2 large tablespoons of baking soda into the bottle.
2. Place the bottle in the pan.
3. Shape the dirt around the bottle to form a mountain. Do not cover the bottle's mouth, and do not get dirt inside the bottle.
4. Color the vinegar with red food coloring; then, using the funnel, pour the liquid into the bottle.

 SAFETY NOTE: This reaction is a bit messy, so be careful. The food coloring will stain clothing. You might want to wear a smock, workshirt, or apron while conducting this experiment.

Explanation

A chemical reaction between the baking soda and the vinegar produces carbon dioxide. This gas builds up enough pressure to force the mixture out of the bottle.

HAUNTED NICKEL

ACTIVITY-AT-A-GLANCE

Purpose

Demonstrates thermal expansion of gases.

When to Use

Curricular Area	Difficulty Level	Time to Do

Gas Formation; Temperature Changes

3 minutes
(plus freezing time)

What You'll Need

- ❏ 12- or 16-ounce glass soda bottle
- ❏ 1 nickel (coin)
- ❏ Freezer
- ❏ Water
- ❏ Table

What to Do

1. Place the empty bottle in the freezer for about 15 to 20 minutes.

2. Remove the bottle and quickly place it on the table in front of you.

3. Quickly moisten the opening of the bottle with water and place the nickel on top of the bottle.

4. Cup your hands around the bottle for 1 to 2 minutes. Do not move or shake the bottle.

5. Observe what the nickel does.

Explanation

The nickel will pop up and down a few times, making a clanking sound. By putting the bottle in the freezer, you are cooling the air inside. Your warm hand reheats the air, which starts to expand. Thermal expansion is when air takes up more space when heated. The nickel acts as a one-way valve. The reheated air breaks the seal, allowing the air to escape. This causes the nickel on the bottle top to mysteriously pop up and down.

JACK FROST'S SECRET MESSAGE

ACTIVITY-AT-A-GLANCE

Purpose

Demonstrates the crystallizing of salt.

When to Use

Curricular Area	Difficulty Level	Time to Do

Physical Change; Crystal Formation

2

10 minutes
(plus drying time)

What You'll Need

- ❑ 1½ cups of water
- ❑ 1½ cups of Epsom salts (available at drugstores)
- ❑ Saucepan
- ❑ Long-tipped cotton swabs
- ❑ Dark-colored construction paper
- ❑ Heat source (stove)

What to Do

1. Mix the water and the Epsom salts in the saucepan.
2. Heat the mixture on the burner until the salt is completely dissolved.
3. Let the mixture cool.
4. Dip the cotton swab into the mixture and write a message on the construction paper.
5. Set the paper aside to dry and watch your secret message appear.

Explanation

The salt will appear as frost-like white crystals on your paper. As the water evaporates, the salt crystallizes and outlines the words or drawings formed on the paper. The dark-colored paper will show the contrast much better than a light-colored paper. (Epsom salts are actually made from a chemical called magnesium sulfate.)

MAGIC SMOKE RINGS

ACTIVITY-AT-A-GLANCE

Purpose

Demonstrates the characteristics of dry ice.

When to Use

Curricular Area	Difficulty Level	Time to Do
Temperature; Phase Changes	3	 5 minutes

What You'll Need

- ❏ 12-ounce clear plastic cup (flexible)
- ❏ Small piece of dry ice (available at ice cream shops)
- ❏ Ice tongs
- ❏ Piece of cardboard to fit on top of the cup
- ❏ Scissors
- ❏ Water
- ❏ Food coloring (optional)

What to Do

1. Fill the cup halfway with water.

2. Add a drop or two of food coloring to the water for effect.

3. Using the ice tongs, place a marble-size piece of dry ice in the cup.

4. Place the cardboard on top of the cup.

5. Cut a round ($^1\!/_2$-inch diameter) hole in the center of the cardboard.

6. Gently squeeze the cup while holding the cardboard in place and observe the misty smoke rings.

 <u>SAFETY NOTE</u>: Do NOT touch the dry ice with your hand. It can cause frostbite.

Explanation

With practice, each squeeze of the cup can generate a beautiful, misty smoke ring that follows a short trajectory path. This is due to the fairly high density of the carbon dioxide-filled mist. Dry ice is simply frozen carbon dioxide. Note that dry ice should not touch exposed skin. The "burning" feeling that results from touching dry ice is not from heat. The intense cold will cause frostbite on exposed skin.

Variation

Try cutting different shapes (round, triangular, etc.) and using them as extra cardboard tops for the cup. You will notice, however, that the misty smoke rings always come out round.

FIREPROOF MONEY

ACTIVITY-AT-A-GLANCE

Purpose

Demonstrates that alcohol is flammable.

When to Use

Curricular Area	Difficulty Level	Time to Do
Combustion; Density	4	**2 minutes**

What You'll Need

- ❏ 1 cup of rubbing alcohol
- ❏ Water
- ❏ A dollar bill
- ❏ Medium-size container
- ❏ Tweezers
- ❏ Matches

What to Do

1. Mix exactly 1 cup of rubbing alcohol with 1 cup of water in the container. Stir well.

2. Using the tweezers, dip the ENTIRE dollar bill in the mixture. Let it sit there for a few seconds.

3. While carefully holding the bill with the tweezers, light the bill with the match. Keep the jar of alcohol closed and the mixing container far away from the open flame.

4. Allow the alcohol to burn off the dollar bill for about 5 to 8 seconds (or less if you see any of the dollar bill burn). Be prepared to smother the flame.

 SAFETY NOTE: Teacher demonstration only. Caution is advised. Work over a fireproof table and wear safety goggles. Keep your face away from the solution. (Alcohol evaporates quickly and inhaling fumes can be dangerous.)

Explanation

The alcohol forms a thin coating on the dollar bill. Since alcohol is flammable, and less dense than the water, it stays on top of the money and burns very fast. The dollar bill should not burn because the alcohol was not absorbed into the tight, woven fibers of the currency. Regular paper will not work well for this activity because the alcohol is more apt to be quickly absorbed into the loose knit fibers of the paper.

OLD RUSTY

 ACTIVITY-AT-A-GLANCE

Purpose

Demonstrates a chemical reaction that creates rust.

When to Use

Curricular Area	Difficulty Level	Time to Do
 Oxidation; Chemical Changes	3	 5 minutes

What You'll Need

- ❏ Small piece of steel wool
- ❏ Clean glass jar
- ❏ 4 tablespoons of liquid bleach
- ❏ 2 tablespoons of vinegar
- ❏ Spoon

What to Do

1. Place the steel wool in the jar.
2. Add the bleach and vinegar.
3. Stir with the spoon for about 5 minutes to create the reaction.

 SAFETY NOTE: Use caution when working with bleach. Wear safety goggles.

Explanation

The red powder you see at the bottom of the jar is actually rust—the chemical term for which is iron oxide. The chemical reaction that occurred between the bleach, vinegar, and iron in the steel wool is known as oxidation. Steel wool rusts because of the iron in the steel wool combining with oxygen.

OXYGEN EATER

ACTIVITY-AT-A-GLANCE

Purpose

Illustrates how decomposition of a substance emits oxygen gas.

When to Use

Curricular Area	Difficulty Level	Time to Do

Chemical Changes

5 minutes

What You'll Need

- ❏ Bottle of 3%-solution hydrogen peroxide
- ❏ Glass jar
- ❏ Package of fresh, dry yeast
- ❏ Craft stick
- ❏ Matches

What to Do

1. Place a few ounces of the hydrogen peroxide in the jar.
2. Sprinkle some yeast in the jar and mix.
3. Make a glowing splint by lighting the tip of the wooden craft stick with the match and then blowing out the flame. There should be a red "glow" at the end of the stick.
4. Place the glowing splint into the mouth of the jar, near the top of the bubbles. The flame should relight.

 SAFETY NOTE: Teacher demonstration only. Work over a fireproof table.

Explanation

The chemical reaction between the yeast and the hydrogen peroxide is called decomposition, because it breaks the bonds of the hydrogen peroxide molecules and releases free oxygen. The yeast caused the hydrogen peroxide to release one oxygen atom above the surface. Since oxygen is flammable, it caused the glowing splint to relight.

A HOMEMADE BATTERY

 ACTIVITY-AT-A-GLANCE

Purpose

Demonstrates how an electric current flows through a home-made battery.

When to Use

Curricular Area	Difficulty Level	Time to Do

Electricity

5 minutes

What You'll Need

- ❏ 6 tablespoons of table salt
- ❏ Small glass or cup
- ❏ Water
- ❏ Heavy-duty (thick) aluminum foil
- ❏ Paper towels

- ❏ Two 8-inch pieces of copper wire
- ❏ Scissors
- ❏ 4 pennies

What to Do

1. Make a salt-water (saline) solution by mixing the table salt with a cup of water.

2. Cut out 4 penny-size pieces of aluminum foil.

3. Cut a paper towel into 4 pieces, somewhat bigger than the foil pieces.

4. Soak the paper towel pieces in the solution for a few seconds.

5. Sandwich a piece of the saturated paper towel between a foil piece and a penny, with the foil at the bottom. Tape the bare end of one wire to the penny.

6. Create 3 more piles (repeating Step 5 three more times) and stack the piles, creating an electric sandwich or voltaic pile.

7. Tape the bare end of the first wire to the copper bottom of your pile and the bare end of the second wire to the aluminum top of your pile.

8. To make your homemade battery work, carefully lift the pile to your mouth. Take the free end of each wire and place both of them—simultaneously—very lightly on your tongue.

 SAFETY NOTE: Warn students they will feel a tingling sensation on their tongues. Each student should have his or her own "battery."

Explanation

In your voltaic pile, a chemical reaction between the two metals (aluminum and copper) caused a weak current of electricity. The current flowed from one wire through your tongue to the other wire, with your tongue acting as a conductor. This is one way a battery is made, with layers of different types of metals stacked together and the addition of a conducting liquid (salt-water, in this case).

THE CHEM-MYSTERY OF FLOATING MOTHBALLS

 ACTIVITY-AT-A-GLANCE

Purpose

Demonstrates how the density of mothballs can change.

When to Use

Curricular Area	Difficulty Level	Time to Do

Density; Chemical Change

10 minutes

What You'll Need

- ❏ 3 mothballs
- ❏ 1 tablespoon of vinegar
- ❏ 1 tablespoon of baking soda
- ❏ Glass of water

What to Do

1. Add the vinegar and the baking soda to the glass of water.
2. Place the mothballs in the liquid and allow several minutes to pass.
3. Observe the change in density.

Explanation

At first, the mothballs sink since they are denser than water. The vinegar and baking soda combine chemically to make bubbles of carbon dioxide gas. The bubbles collect on the mothballs, causing them to float to the top. While the mothballs are floating at the top, some of the bubbles of gas burst into the air, causing the mothballs to lose some of their buoyancy. This sinking and floating continues until the vinegar and baking soda stop producing carbon dioxide.

WHO DONE IT?

 ACTIVITY-AT-A-GLANCE

Purpose

Shows a fingerprinting method.

When to Use

Curricular Area	Difficulty Level	Time to Do

Body Oils and Surface Reactions

2

5 minutes

What You'll Need

- ❑ Glass microscope slide or small mirror (or another smooth, glassy surface)
- ❑ Baby powder or plain talcum powder
- ❑ Small, soft brush
- ❑ Clear (not "invisible") adhesive tape
- ❑ 3-inch square of glossy black paper

What to Do

1. Press your thumb firmly against the glass slide or other glassy surface.

2. Hold the glass by the edges and examine it for your thumbprint.

3. Gently sprinkle a little of the powder onto the brush and wipe it across the glass. Observe the thumbprint.

4. Cut a piece of tape bigger than the thumbprint and gently put the sticky side of the tape onto the dusted thumbprint.

5. Carefully and slowly peel the tape off the glass.

6. Stick the tape to the black paper. You now have a copy of your thumbprint.

Explanation

Whenever you touch anything, you leave a tiny amount of oil from your skin on whatever you touched with your hand. This oil comes off in the pattern of the ridges of your fingertips. That's a fingerprint!

SECTION TWO

KITCHEN SCIENCE

When most people go into their kitchens, the last thing they probably think about is science. After you and your classes dabble with the activities in this section, however, your students will have a whole new perspective. Some interesting chemical reactions can take place in the food preparation area. Using items ranging from bananas and nuts to cereal and milk, your students are going to get very hungry—hungry for science, that is.

BUTTER BEATERS

 ACTIVITY-AT-A-GLANCE

Purpose

Demonstrates the creation of butter from cream.

When to Use

Curricular Area	Difficulty Level	Time to Do

Mixtures and Solutions

1

5 minutes

What You'll Need

- ❏ Small glass jar with lid
- ❏ Heavy whipping cream
- ❏ Several small marbles

SkyLight Training and Publishing Inc.

What to Do

1. Fill the jar about $^1/_2$ full with the whipping cream.
2. Place the marbles into the jar and secure the lid.
3. Carefully shake the container for several minutes. Observe.

 <u>SAFETY NOTE</u>: Advise students not to eat this butter unless they are working with very clean equipment and fresh whipping cream.

Explanation

The marbles hitting the fat molecules in the whipping cream resulted in agitation, which caused the particles from the cream to separate and mix with the air particles. The result was the formation of butter.

Variation

Try the same activity using instant pudding mix and milk instead of whipping cream.

NUTTY CANDLE

 ## ACTIVITY-AT-A-GLANCE

Purpose

Demonstrates a way to look at the chemical process of burning.

When to Use

Curricular Area	Difficulty Level	Time to Do
Chemical and Heat Reactions	**3**	 **1 minute**

What You'll Need

- ❏ Small paring knife
- ❏ Banana
- ❏ Sliver of almond or pecan (elongated; shaped roughly like a candlewick)
- ❏ Matches or lighter

What to Do

1. Take the banana and, using the knife, shape the top of the banana so that it resembles the top of a candle.
2. Place the sliver of the nut in the top of the banana.
3. Light the nut with the matches. It may take a few tries for it to ignite.
4. Let the "candle" burn for a few moments.

 SAFETY NOTE: This activity should be handled as a teacher demonstration or conducted with the help of an adult. Be prepared to douse the flame.

Explanation

The nut burns because all nuts have a very high oil content and oil burns. The black material on the burnt nut is carbon. Carbon is one of the elements that make up all organisms. Note that you may want to set up this experiment in the classroom beforehand and turn the lights off for a special effect during class.

EATING IRON, YUM!

ACTIVITY-AT-A-GLANCE

Purpose

Illustrates that certain foods (iron-fortified cereals, in this case) contain iron.

When to Use

Curricular Area	Difficulty Level	Time to Do

Health; Chemical Changes

5 minutes
(plus 20 minutes of stirring time)

What You'll Need

- ❏ Small magnetic bar (for stirring)
- ❏ Large, plastic container
- ❏ 2 cups of any brand of breakfast cereal that contains 100% of the minimum daily requirement of iron
- ❏ Water, enough to cover the cereal
- ❏ Wooden spoon

What to Do

1. Place the magnetic stirring bar into the container.
2. Crush the cereal between your hands as you add it to the container.
3. Add enough water to cover the cereal. Stir with the wooden spoon to make a thin slush.
4. Stir the slush gently for 20 minutes with the magnetic bar. (Someone else can help by taking a turn stirring.)
5. Remove the magnetic stirring bar and observe the iron (powder from the cereal) attached to the bar.

Explanation

Iron is an important element in human nutrition, so many cereals are iron-fortified—as the experiment demonstrates. Iron deficiency is the most common form of malnutrition in the United States. Iron is absorbed into the human body most effectively when the iron is ingested with vitamin C.

EGG POWER

  ACTIVITY-AT-A-GLANCE

Purpose

Demonstrates the strength of eggshells.

When to Use

Curricular Area	Difficulty Level	Time to Do
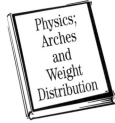 Physics; Arches and Weight Distribution		 **3 minutes**

What You'll Need

- ❑ 2 uncooked eggs (4 empty eggshell halves)
- ❑ Masking tape
- ❑ Scissors
- ❑ Several books

SkyLight Training and Publishing Inc.

What to Do

1. Carefully crack open 2 uncooked eggs so that you have 4 empty eggshells.

2. Clean out the eggshell halves. Wrap a piece of masking tape around the middle of each empty eggshell half.

3. With the scissors, trim off the excess shell so that each half has a straight-edged bottom.

4. Lay out the 4 eggshells (domes up) so that they form a square.

5. Now carefully lay the first book, face down, on the 4 eggshells. Continue to carefully stack books on top of one another until the shells crack.

 SAFETY NOTE: Use caution when trimming the eggshells with the scissors.

Explanation

Eggshells can support a good deal of weight. They will not crack right away. The secret of their strength is their shape. In this experiment the weight is evenly distributed among all 4 eggshell halves, that weight being carried down along the arches (the curved tops of the eggs) to the base of the square.

POTATO POWER

ACTIVITY-AT-A-GLANCE

Purpose

Illustrates the power of air pressure.

When to Use

Curricular Area	Difficulty Level	Time to Do

Force; Air Pressure

1 minute

What You'll Need

- ❏ A small, fresh (uncooked), unpeeled potato
- ❏ Plastic drinking straw

SkyLight Training and Publishing Inc.

What to Do

1. Hold the straw in the center and try to poke it through the potato.
2. Now cover the top end of the straw with your finger and try again to stick the straw through the potato. Use quick, steady jabs.
3. Observe that you will be able to get the bottom section of the straw all the way through a fresh potato. (If this doesn't work the first time, keep trying.)

Explanation

The straw will pierce the potato only when one end of the straw is closed up—that is, when your finger traps a volume of air inside the straw. This trapped air is strong enough (along with the force you place on the straw) to allow you to pierce the potato.

HOW NOW, BROWN COW?

 ACTIVITY-AT-A-GLANCE

Purpose

Demonstrates how milk can be separated into its solid and liquid parts.

When to Use

Curricular Area	Difficulty Level	Time to Do

Mixtures and Solutions; Chemical Reactions

3 minutes

What You'll Need

- ❏ Small jar with a lid
- ❏ Fresh whole milk
- ❏ 2 tablespoons of vinegar

What to Do

1. Fill the jar ³/₄ full of milk.
2. Add 2 tablespoons of vinegar
3. Allow the jar to sit for a few minutes.

Explanation

The solid particles in the milk are evenly spread throughout the liquid. The vinegar, which is a weak acid, causes the small undissolved particles to clump together and form the solid curd. The liquid that remains is the whey. Milk is an example of a colloid, which is a mixture of liquids and small particles.

I SCREAM FOR ICE CREAM

ACTIVITY-AT-A-GLANCE

Purpose

Demonstrates a change in energy and matter.

When to Use

Curricular Area	Difficulty Level	Time to Do
Physical Changes; Phase Change	3	20 minutes

What You'll Need

- ❏ 1 gallon-size zip-type plastic freezer bag
- ❏ Crushed ice
- ❏ 1 pint-size (about $6^5/_8$ x $5^7/_8$-inch) zip-type plastic bag
- ❏ 6 tablespoons of salt
- ❏ $1/_2$ cup milk
- ❏ 1 tablespoon of sugar
- ❏ $1/_2$ teaspoon of vanilla

SkyLight Training and Publishing Inc.

What to Do

1. Place the crushed ice in the gallon freezer bag, filling it halfway.
2. Add the salt to the large bag and shake it.
3. Seal the bag while squeezing out the excess air.
4. Put the milk, vanilla, and sugar into the small freezer bag. Seal the bag while squeezing out the air.
5. Place the sealed, smaller bag into the large bag.
6. Shake the bags for about 5 to 10 minutes until the mixture reaches a thick appearance like soft-serve ice cream.
7. Open the large bag, then remove the small bag, and enjoy your home-made ice cream.

 SAFETY NOTE: Since your students will no doubt want to eat their ice cream, advise them to use clean equipment and fresh ingredients for this activity.

Explanation

While you were making your ice cream, you observed a physical change in matter: The ice and salt melted to a liquid and absorbed heat energy from the liquid/milk mixture, which was warmer. This, in turn, caused the milk mixture to cool. As energy (heat) was being removed, the liquid turned into a solid. Observing the freezing process in this activity helps visualize the principle that heat energy always flows "downhill" into cooler materials.

Variation

Use whole, low-fat, and no-fat milk varieties for this activity and compare end results in terms of consistency (creaminess).

INSTANT MOUSSE

ACTIVITY-AT-A-GLANCE

Purpose

Demonstrates how a polymer can be made from common food products.

When to Use

Curricular Area	Difficulty Level	Time to Do

Chemical Reactions; Gas Formation

5 minutes

What You'll Need

- ❏ 2 eggs
- ❏ Water
- ❏ Plastic cup
- ❏ Baking soda
- ❏ Crystallized citric acid (available in the food preserving section of supermarkets)

SkyLight Training and Publishing Inc.

What to Do

1. Separate egg whites from yolks. Discard yolks.
2. In a cup, mix together equal amounts of egg whites and water.
3. Add a generous amount of baking soda.
4. Sprinkle citric acid over the mixture and stir together.
5. Turn your "mousse" upside down.

 SAFETY NOTE: Caution students not to eat this mousse since un-cooked eggs can harbor salmonella bacteria.

Explanation

This is a good example of a chemical reaction that takes place every day in the kitchen. The baking soda releases carbon dioxide, which causes the egg white/water combination to inflate. The citric acid neutralizes the baking soda and acts as a thickener.

INVISIBLE FRUIT INK

ACTIVITY-AT-A-GLANCE

Purpose

Demonstrates how a fruit juice breaks down chemically.

When to Use

Curricular Area	Difficulty Level	Time to Do
 Chemical Breakdown of Organisms		 **3 minutes** (plus drying time)

What You'll Need

- ❏ Any type of fruit juice (orange, grapefruit, apple, etc.)
- ❏ Paintbrush with a fine tip
- ❏ Plastic cup
- ❏ Notebook paper
- ❏ Lamp with a 75-watt (or greater) light bulb

What to Do

1. Place a small amount of juice in a plastic cup.
2. Dip the paintbrush in the juice. Use the brush to write a secret message on a piece of notebook paper.
3. Allow the paper and "ink" to dry (about 20 to 30 minutes).
4. Turn on the lamp, and hold the paper over the light bulb until the message is readable.

 SAFETY NOTE: Do not touch the light bulb and do not leave the paper on the light bulb.

Explanation

When the juice is heated, the once-living plant materials that make up the beverage break down, producing—among other things—carbon, which is black. Carbon is a basic element that is in all living things, including our bodies.

Variation

Try other liquids such as milk, sugar water, and soft drinks.

LEMON BATTERY

 ACTIVITY-AT-A-GLANCE

Purpose

Displays how a battery works.

When to Use

Curricular Area	Difficulty Level	Time to Do

 Electricity; Conduction

5 minutes

What You'll Need

- ❏ Small (metal) paper clip
- ❏ Piece of noninsulated copper wire
- ❏ Wire cutters
- ❏ Fresh, whole lemon

What to Do

1. Straighten out the paper clip and copper wire. They should be the same lengths. Trim, if necessary.
2. Stick both wires deep into the lemon, side by side, about ½-inch apart.
3. Gently place the free ends of both wires on your tongue.

 SAFETY NOTE: Warn students they will feel a tingling sensation on their tongues. Each student should have his or her own "lemon battery."

Explanation

You received a slight tingle on your tongue with your homemade battery because electrons, which are negatively charged particles that make up electricity, passed through your saliva onto your tongue. The citric acid (the juice) in the lemon acted as a conductor of electricity. For the lemon battery to complete the circuit, which it did if you felt a tingling sensation on your tongue, two different types of conductive metals (copper and a steel alloy, in this case) are needed.

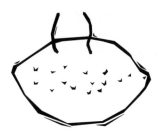

MARSHMALLOW GLACIER

ACTIVITY-AT-A-GLANCE

Purpose

Demonstrates how pressure increases compaction.

When to Use

Curricular Area	Difficulty Level	Time to Do

Glacier Formation; Pressure

2

5 minutes

What You'll Need

- ❏ Thick, tall, clear plastic glass
- ❏ 6 to 8 regular-size marshmallows
- ❏ Small piece of cardboard
- ❏ Scissors
- ❏ Set of small weights

SkyLight Training and Publishing Inc.

What to Do

1. Stack the marshmallows in the plastic glass.
2. Cut out a cardboard disk (circle) to fit snugly inside the glass.
3. Place the cardboard disk on top of the marshmallows.
4. Place the weights, one at a time, on top of the disk.

Explanation

As the marshmallows start to push together, the lower layers are more compact due to the additional weight on them. This is similar to the compacting process and resulting pressure of snow forming a glacier. (You may want to remind students that a glacier is a slow-moving body of ice found in polar climates.) As snow falls, the bottom layers of the glacier have more weight on them and turn to ice. The additional weight adds pressure; therefore, the bottom layers of the glacier are more compacted than the top layers.

Variation

Color the marshmallows with different food colorings for a special effect.

THIS IS NUTS!

ACTIVITY-AT-A-GLANCE

Purpose

Demonstrates that no two pieces of matter can occupy the same space at the same time.

When to Use

Curricular Area	Difficulty Level	Time to Do

Molecular Motion

2

3 minutes

What You'll Need

- ❑ 1 quart glass jar with a lid
- ❑ Uncooked rice
- ❑ Whole walnut (in shell)

SkyLight Training and Publishing Inc.

What to Do

1. Fill the jar ³/₄ full with uncooked rice.
2. Place the walnut on top of the rice and close the lid.
3. Hold the jar upright, then turn it upside down.
4. Shake the jar back and forth, sideways, vigorously, until the walnut surfaces on the top. *Do not shake the jar up and down.*

Explanation

There are spaces between the grains of rice. As the jar is shaken, the rice gets closer together. This is known as settling. As the rice vibrates and moves together, it pushes the walnut upward. Molecules vibrate and behave in the same manner.

YEAST BEAST

 ACTIVITY-AT-A-GLANCE

Purpose

Demonstrates how yeast, a fungus, grows.

When to Use

Curricular Area	Difficulty Level	Time to Do

Fungus and Gas Formation

3

25 minutes

What You'll Need

- ❏ 2 zip-type plastic sandwich bags
- ❏ 2 packets of dried baking yeast
- ❏ 1 teaspoon of granular sugar
- ❏ Marker
- ❏ Warm water
- ❏ Measuring cup

SkyLight Training and Publishing Inc.

What to Do

1. Pour 1 packet of yeast into each of the bags.
2. Place the sugar into only one of the bags.
3. Label one bag "SUGAR" and label the other bag "NO SUGAR."
4. Pour $\frac{1}{4}$ cup of warm water into each bag and seal them, carefully squeezing the air out.
5. Holding a bag in each hand, gently shake for 1 minute. Set bags aside.
6. Check the bags every 5 minutes for about 20 minutes.

Explanation

Sugar is a food product and, therefore, will cause the yeast to "grow." As it grows, it produces new yeast plants. In the process, the yeast gives off alcohol and carbon dioxide gas. This gas formation causes the bag to expand. Just adding water is not enough to make it grow. Yeast is a living body (a fungus) and needs energy (sugar/food) to grow.

SECTION THREE

BALLOONS, BUBBLES, AND TOYS

Balloons, bubbles, and plastic toys, common playthings, are actually made up of very complex molecules called polymers. Anything made from plastic is a polymer. In this section, you and your students will have a chance to investigate some of the unusual characteristics of everyday toys. Ask your students to identify the polymers around them as they begin this section.

MAGIC BALLOON

ACTIVITY-AT-A-GLANCE

Purpose

Illustrates the formation of a gas during a chemical reaction.

When to Use

Curricular Area	Difficulty Level	Time to Do
Gas Formation; Chemical Reactions	3	5 minutes

What You'll Need

- ❏ Funnel
- ❏ 16-ounce glass or plastic soda bottle with a narrow neck
- ❏ 12 ounces of vinegar
- ❏ 6- to 8-inch latex balloon
- ❏ ½ cup of baking soda

What to Do

1. Fill the soda bottle with the vinegar, almost to the top.

2. Place the small end of the funnel in the opening of the balloon. Pour the baking soda into the balloon. Carefully remove the funnel.

3. Pinch the base of the neck of the balloon and carefully stretch it over the mouth of the bottle. Be careful not to allow the baking soda to spill into the bottle just yet.

4. Now, while holding the balloon upright, allow the baking soda to drop into the vinegar. Hold the balloon in place on the bottle as the bubbling occurs. (Some vinegar will go into the balloon, but in a few moments it will fall back into the bottle.)

5. The balloon will start to inflate. After the balloon has filled up to its maximum with the gas, you may carefully remove it from the bottle and tie to secure it.

Explanation

When baking soda and vinegar mix, carbon dioxide gas is produced in a chemical reaction, causing the balloon to expand. The carbon dioxide gas released into the air causes the bubbling and fizzing. *We exhale carbon dioxide gas with every breath we take.*

A HOMEMADE FLYWHEEL

 ACTIVITY-AT-A-GLANCE

Purpose

Exhibits the principles of inertia and motion.

When to Use

Curricular Area	Difficulty Level	Time to Do
Newton's First Law of Motion	3	 **5 minutes**

What You'll Need

- ❏ String
- ❏ Button with 2 or more holes

What to Do

1. Thread about 2 feet of string through one hole in the button and back through an opposite hole.
2. Tie the string ends together.
3. Center the button in the middle.
4. Hold each end of the string, one end in each hand, and twirl the button until the string and button are tightly wound. (The double strands of the string will be twisted around each other.)
5. Start pulling on the string quickly and the button will spin very rapidly.
6. After the string has untwisted, if you hold it loose and don't move, the button will keep on moving and will wind up again. (However, it will go in the opposite direction.)

Explanation

What you made is called a flywheel. Flywheels abide by the principle that objects at rest tend to remain at rest. Objects in motion tend to keep moving in a straight line (Newton's First Law of Motion). It takes little energy to keep your flywheel moving at a high speed.

Variation

Try different-size buttons and strings for making different flywheels.

CARD SHARK

ACTIVITY-AT-A-GLANCE

Purpose

Proves that force is needed to overcome friction.

When to Use

Curricular Area	Difficulty Level	Time to Do
 Newton's First Law of Motion		 1 minute

What You'll Need

❏ Glass
❏ Playing card
❏ Penny or dime

What to Do

1. Cover the glass with the playing card.
2. Place the coin in the center of the card.
3. Snap the card with your finger so that it flies off the top of the glass. (If you do not get it the first time, practice.) Watch what happens to the coin.

Explanation

The coin will drop directly into the glass because of inertia. An object in motion will continue to move until something stops it and an object at rest will remain at rest until something moves it. This is known as Newton's First Law of Motion.

The card moves because you snap it with your fingers, but the coin will not move because the force of gravity pulls down on it into the glass. Inertia overcame the friction between the card and the glass.

CHEW ON THIS ONE

 ACTIVITY-AT-A-GLANCE

Purpose

Demonstrates how much sugar is in bubble gum.

When to Use

Curricular Area	Difficulty Level	Time to Do

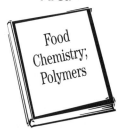

Food Chemistry; Polymers

20 minutes

What You'll Need

- ❏ Bubble gum (not sugarless)
- ❏ Balance that measures to the nearest tenth of a gram—or a fraction of an ounce
- ❏ Small pieces of waxed paper

What to Do

1. Weigh 1 piece of bubble gum and record the results.
2. Chew the gum for exactly 10 minutes.
3. Place the gum on the waxed paper and weigh the piece again.
4. Subtract the second weight from the first weight. That is how much sugar is in the gum (considering that weight of the saliva added during chewing is nominal). Using the data gathered, calculate the percentage of sugar that was in the gum before chewing.

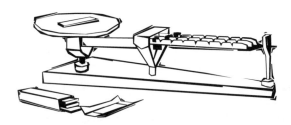

Explanation

Bubble gum, which generally has more sugar than other chewing gum, is made from several ingredients including sugar and a latex polymer. This latex gives the bubble gum the elasticity and strength needed to blow large bubbles. The digestive juices in a person's mouth change the sugar into glucose, which is then absorbed into the body.

Variation

Repeat the steps above with other brands of gum, including regular chewing gum—not just bubble gum. Sugarless gum can also be used for this activity since the artificial sweetener—which does dissolve during chewing—is a weight factor, although not as much as sugar is in regular gum.

DUELING BALLOONS

ACTIVITY-AT-A-GLANCE

Purpose

Demonstrates what happens when two identical objects share the same space (air).

When to Use

Curricular Area	Difficulty Level	Time to Do

Properties of a Gas; Gas Laws

2 minutes

What You'll Need

❏ 2 identical balloons, stretched out well
❏ 2 pincher-type clothespins
❏ Empty spool of thread with a single hole through the center

---

What to Do

1. Inflate one of the balloons almost to its maximum capacity.
2. Twist the balloon's neck and clamp it with a clothespin so that no air escapes.
3. Place the open neck of the balloon over one end of the spool.
4. Inflate the second balloon to about a quarter of the size of the first balloon.
5. Clamp it with the second clothespin and place its neck over the other end of the spool.
6. Remove both clothespins at the same time.

Explanation

The air flows from the smaller balloon to the bigger balloon because there is more air pressure in the smaller one. This is the same principle used by utility companies to deliver natural gas to our homes from hundreds if not thousands of miles away. After the gas is pumped underground, it is put under high pressure so it can flow inside the pipelines.

Variation

You may try this experiment using a 2-inch length of plastic tubing (1/2-inch diameter) instead of a spool. Also, you may inflate the second balloon to half the size of the first. Then try the experiment with both balloons inflated to the same size.

HAVE A BALL

 ACTIVITY-AT-A-GLANCE

Purpose

Illustrates changing potential energy to kinetic energy.

When to Use

Curricular Area	Difficulty Level	Time to Do
 Transfer of Energy		
		1 minute

What You'll Need

❑ Tennis ball
❑ Volleyball

What to Do

1. Drop the tennis ball to the floor from shoulder height.
2. Do the same with the volleyball.
3. Now place the tennis ball on top of the volleyball and drop both simultaneously.

Explanation

The tennis ball rebounds much higher when dropped with the volleyball, because the volleyball has already hit the floor first and is moving back up by the time it hits the tennis ball. This is an example of the transfer of potential energy (stationary energy) to kinetic energy (motion energy).

Variation

Ask a friend to measure the heights of the bounces with a yardstick or meterstick as you perform the experiment.

HELIUM ICE CUBE

 ACTIVITY-AT-A-GLANCE

Purpose

Demonstrates how cold air and warm air interact with molecules within a polymer.

When to Use

Curricular Area	Difficulty Level	Time to Do

5 minutes

What You'll Need

- ❏ 1 helium-filled latex balloon
- ❏ Freezer

SkyLight Training and Publishing Inc.

What to Do

1. Place the balloon in the freezer (or take it outside on a very cold day—under 30° Fahrenheit) for about 5 minutes.
2. Take the balloon out of the freezer and bring it back into the room. Notice its size.

Explanation

When the balloon is put in the freezer, the cold air makes the molecules move more slowly. Therefore, the balloon appears deflated, although the amount of helium in the balloon never changed. When the balloon is back to room temperature, the molecules move faster and the balloon resumes its original size and shape. Since the balloon material is a polymer, it is very flexible and will expand and contract with the change in temperature and with the movement of molecules.

INDY 500

ACTIVITY-AT-A-GLANCE

Purpose

Demonstrates how a polymer can be a powerful force.

When to Use

Curricular Area	Difficulty Level	Time to Do
Newton's First Law of Motion	2	 5 minutes

What You'll Need

❏ Lightweight, plastic toy car with 4 movable wheels
❏ Clean, smooth surface such as a desk
❏ Long balloon (about 10 inches)
❏ Adhesive tape

What to Do

1. Place the toy car on a smooth surface.
2. Inflate the balloon, pinching the neck of the balloon to keep it inflated. Attach a long piece of tape over the balloon and tape the balloon onto the back of the car, with the opening of the balloon facing the rear of the car.
3. Release the neck of the balloon, allowing it to deflate, and observe the car.

Explanation

The balloon exerted a force to the car, causing it to move across the table. This force came from air you placed in the balloon that, upon release, pushed the car forward. This is a good example of Newton's First Law of Motion, inertia: An object stays at rest or remains in motion until acted upon by an outside force. This experiment also demonstrates Newton's Third Law of Motion: For every action, there is an opposite and equal reaction. The air shooting backwards pushed the car forward.

JET ENGINE BALLOON

ACTIVITY-AT-A-GLANCE

Purpose

Shows the principles of jet propulsion.

When to Use

Curricular Area	Difficulty Level	Time to Do
Air Pressure; Newton's Third Law of Motion	2	5 minutes

What You'll Need

- ❏ 10 feet of thick thread or smooth string
- ❏ Plastic drinking straw
- ❏ 2 sturdy chairs or other movable pieces of furniture
- ❏ Long balloon (about 10 inches)
- ❏ Adhesive tape

SkyLight Training and Publishing Inc.

What to Do

1. Push one end of the string though the straw.
2. Tie one end of the string to one of the chairs.
3. Stretch the string across the room and tie it the other chair.
4. Pull on the second chair and make the string very taut, but do not pull on the string so hard that you break it.
5. Blow up the balloon and hold the end so the air doesn't escape.
6. Tape the balloon onto the straw with 2 pieces of tape, using one strip of tape in front and one in back. Make sure that the balloon doesn't deflate.
7. Move the balloon-straw combination back to the end of the chair. Make sure the end of the balloon you are holding is pointed away from the long end of the string.
8. Release the balloon and observe.

Explanation

When you let go of the balloon, the air pushed the balloon forward. What causes a jet engine to move is a change in air pressure. This is the same type of action and reaction that moved the balloon down the string. This experiment demonstrates Newton's third law of motion: When an object exerts a force upon another object, the second object exerts an equal and opposite force upon the first object. The action in a jet engine is the exhaust from the engine; the reaction is the jet moving forward. Jets need oxygen to burn fuel, which gives the engine energy. In the case of this balloon experiment, the energy came from your breath.

Variation

Set up several balloons on the same string track. Use different-sized balloons.

MAGIC BUBBLES

ACTIVITY-AT-A-GLANCE

Purpose

Demonstrates the properties of soap film, bubbles, and surface tension.

When to Use

Curricular Area

Physical Properties; Surface Tension

Difficulty Level

Time to Do

10 minutes

What You'll Need

- ❏ Metal coat hanger (to make the wand)
- ❏ String
- ❏ Tray (about 8 x 10-inches)
- ❏ Liquid bubbles, which can be made by mixing 2 cups of dishwashing liquid, 1 cup of glycerin (available in drugstores), and 3 cups of water

What to Do

1. Make a wand by bending the coat hanger into a loop. Twist the ends together, leaving a few inches for a handle. Make sure the "wand" will fit into the tray.

2. Loosely wrap the string around the coat hanger edges. This will help hold the bubbles in place.

3. Pour the bubble solution into the tray.

4. Dip your wand into the tray and start blowing bubbles.

Explanation

The soap contains a long chain of hydrocarbon molecules with oxygen attached. When you add water to the soap, the soap will move toward the surface. The soap reduces the tension and adds elastic properties. When the wand is dipped in the solution, the water drains from inside the raised surface, making the surface collapse on itself and form a layered film.

Variation

To save time, you can buy liquid bubbles at a supermarket or toy store. To extend the activity, you can make moving bubbles by using 2 soda straws and 2 feet of string. Run the string through the straws and tie the ends together. Form a rectangle with the wand and dip it into the soap. The film will coat the wand and can be gently moved a few inches side to side.

MY POP IS BIGGER THAN YOUR POP

ACTIVITY-AT-A-GLANCE

Purpose

Demonstrates how color can be used to predict when a bubble will pop.

When to Use

Curricular Area	Difficulty Level	Time to Do

Surface Tension; Physical Changes

1

10 minutes

What You'll Need

- ❏ Liquid dishwashing soap
- ❏ Measuring cup
- ❏ Water
- ❏ Gallon container
- ❏ Glycerin (optional; available at drugstores)
- ❏ Straw
- ❏ Watch or clock with second hand

What to Do

1. Mix ¹/₂ gallon of water and ¹/₂ cup of liquid soap in a gallon container.
2. For extra strong bubbles, add a few ounces of glycerin.
3. Pour a small amount of the bubble solution on a flat surface.
4. Place the straw at an angle and gently blow into the solution, forming a bubble.
5. After blowing a medium-size bubble, take the straw from the solution and observe the colors on the surface of the bubble as it sits on the straw.
6. When the bubble turns black in some areas, start timing. Your bubble will pop in approximately 3 to 4 seconds.

Explanation

The surface tension of the bubble gets very thin before it breaks. As this surface gets thinner, it reflects less light. This small amount of light is black, which by definition is the combination of all colors.

WACKY SPACE SHUTTLE

ACTIVITY-AT-A-GLANCE

Purpose

Shows how pressure increases when gas is produced.

When to Use

Curricular Area	Difficulty Level	Time to Do
 Air Pressure; Gas Formation		 5 minutes

What You'll Need

❑ Clear, plastic 2-liter soda bottle
❑ $\frac{1}{2}$ cup of vinegar
❑ 2 tablespoons of baking soda
❑ Piece of facial tissue or toilet paper
❑ Cork that will fit the 2-liter bottle (the rocket)

SkyLight Training and Publishing Inc.

What to Do

1. Pour the vinegar in the soda bottle.
2. Place the baking soda on a piece of facial tissue. Wrap the baking soda in the tissue tight enough so that this bundle will fit through the neck of the bottle.
3. Tilt the bottle at a slight angle and place the bundle into it.
4. Place the cork firmly (but not too tightly) into the neck of the bottle, and allow the bundle to drop into the vinegar. Stand the bottle erect or place it at a slight angle, aimed away from any people. Wait for the "launch" signal.

 SAFETY NOTE: This activity should be a teacher demonstration or, at least, be adult-monitored. Warn students NOT to aim the bottle with the cork in it at anyone. *Perform this activity outdoors.*

Explanation

As the liquid slowly soaks through the tissue paper, the reaction of the baking soda and vinegar produces carbon dioxide gas. As more gas forms, pressure increases in the closed container until it is great enough to force the cork out of the bottle.

Variation

Attach a few streamers or pieces of ribbon to the cork for a colorful effect.

CANNON POWER

 ACTIVITY-AT-A-GLANCE

Purpose

Demonstrates the flexibility of polymers and how this flexibility applies to air pressure.

When to Use

Curricular Area	Difficulty Level	Time to Do
 Polymers; Pressure		 **5 minutes**

What You'll Need

- ❏ Clean 1- or 2-lb. coffee can (empty) with plastic lid
- ❏ Can opener
- ❏ Scissors
- ❏ Large balloon
- ❏ Rubber bands
- ❏ Candle in candleholder
- ❏ Matches

What to Do

1. Remove the bottom of the coffee can with the can opener.
2. Cut a hole about the size of a quarter in the center of the plastic lid.
3. Put the lid on one end of the can.
4. Cut the balloon open so it can be stretched over the other end of the can. Secure the balloon with the rubberbands. You have now made your "cannon." (The balloon material should be very tight, but flexible.)
5. Light the candle and set it about 6 inches away from your cannon.
6. Place your cannon, with the lid toward the flame, so that it is even with the candle. (The quarter-size opening in the lid should be directly in front of the flame.)
7. Flick your finger in the back of the cannon. Hit the balloon with enough force to extinguish the flame.

 SAFETY NOTE: Teacher demonstration only.

Explanation

The candle blew out because as you tapped on the flexible balloon you decreased the volume of air that was trapped inside the can. The excess air in the can was forced out through the small opening. The rapid force of that air being removed from the can extinguished the flame. Note that both the plastic lid and the balloon are polymers.

WATER/AIR BALLOON

ACTIVITY-AT-A-GLANCE

Purpose

Demonstrates center of gravity with air and water.

When to Use

Curricular Area	Difficulty Level	Time to Do

Gravity

3

2 minutes

What You'll Need

- ❏ 1 small round balloon
- ❏ Water
- ❏ 1 large round balloon

SkyLight Training and Publishing Inc.

What to Do

1. Fill the small balloon with a small amount of water and tie it.
2. Gently push the water-filled balloon inside the large balloon. This can be difficult, so you may need some help from a friend.
3. Blow up the large balloon and tie it.
4. Play "catch" with the water/air balloon with your friend.

Explanation

The water/air balloon wobbles as it is thrown because its center of gravity moves around as it flies through the air. The balloon's center of gravity is the water-filled balloon.

Variation

Try different-sized balloons filled with water and air.

SECTION FOUR

HOT AND COLD STUFF

Most people live in climates where there are variations in temperature, ranging from hot to cold. For many of us, the seasons bring distinct changes: Temperatures will vary from hot to mild to cold and then back again. For many, temperature is a significant factor in life. People will often check the thermometer or weather reports to decide how to dress for the day. In this section, you and your students will take a look at hot and cold from different perspectives.

A CUT ABOVE

 ACTIVITY-AT-A-GLANCE

Purpose

Illustrates how heat can be intensified.

When to Use

Curricular Area	Difficulty Level	Time to Do

Solar Energy; Optics

3

5 minutes

What You'll Need

- ❏ Piece of string (not thread)
- ❏ Adhesive tape
- ❏ 1 quart glass jar with lid
- ❏ Sunshine
- ❏ Magnifying glass

What to Do

1. Tape the top of the string to the middle of the inside portion of the jar lid.

2. Insert the string in the jar and screw on the lid.

3. With the string hanging in the jar, go outdoors or near a window on a sunny day.

4. Taking the magnifying glass, focus the rays of the sun on the string for a few minutes. Hold the magnifier steadily, aiming at one specific spot on the string until it breaks.

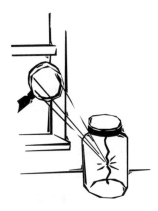

Explanation

The string breaks as the magnifying glass concentrates the heat of the sun on one spot of the string. The heat becomes intense enough to burn right through the string because the magnifying glass is increasing the concentration of the sun's energy to one location.

COLLAPSING BOTTLE

 ACTIVITY-AT-A-GLANCE

Purpose

Illustrates how warm air takes up more space than cold air.

When to Use

Curricular Area	Difficulty Level	Time to Do
Vacuum Formation	3	 **5 minutes**

What You'll Need

- ❏ Stove or other heat source
- ❏ Pan
- ❏ Water
- ❏ Funnel
- ❏ Empty 2-liter plastic soda bottle with cap
- ❏ Sink or pail, to empty water

SkyLight Training and Publishing Inc.

What to Do

1. Heat a pan of water on the stove until it almost boils.
2. Using the funnel, carefully fill the soda bottle about $1/4$ of the way with the hot water.
3. Tightly screw the cap on the bottle.
4. Gently shake the bottle for 30 seconds.
5. Remove the cap and immediately empty the bottle in the sink.
6. Quickly screw the cap back on.
7. Set the bottle down and observe that the bottle collapses.

 SAFETY NOTE: Teacher demonstration only. Use caution when pouring the hot water.

Explanation

The bottle collapses because warm air takes up more space, since its molecules move faster than cold air particles. As the air inside the bottle cools down, the air takes up less space so that the air pressure outside the bottle is greater than air pressure inside the bottle. This causes a partial vacuum on the inside, and you get an implosion—the opposite of an explosion.

COOL IT

ACTIVITY-AT-A-GLANCE

Purpose

Illustrates how evaporation affects the cooling process.

When to Use

Curricular Area	Difficulty Level	Time to Do

Evaporation and Temperature

1

1 minute

What You'll Need

- ❏ Small amount of rubbing alcohol
- ❏ 2 cotton balls
- ❏ Water

What to Do

1. With the cotton ball, dab the back of one hand with the rubbing alcohol.
2. With the other cotton ball, dab the back of your other hand with some water.
3. At the same time, wave both hands in the air and note which hand feels colder.

 SAFETY NOTE: Do not get the alcohol in your eyes or in an open cut; it will burn.

Explanation

Heat is absorbed from the surface of your skin as the water and alcohol evaporate. Therefore, the temperature of your body is lowered. Alcohol evaporates faster than water. The more rapid evaporation of alcohol results in greater coolness. This is why you feel cooler when you step out of the shower or if you get an alcohol rub when you have a high fever.

DEW PROCESS

 ACTIVITY-AT-A-GLANCE

Purpose

Demonstrates how fog and dew are created.

When to Use

Curricular Area	Difficulty Level	Time to Do

Weather

15 minutes

What You'll Need

- ❏ Glass jar with a narrow mouth
- ❏ Cup of very hot tap water
- ❏ Ice cubes
- ❏ Small plastic sandwich bag
- ❏ Medium-size metal can

What to Do

Part A:

1. Pour the hot water into the glass jar.
2. Place the ice cubes in the plastic bag and put the bag over the mouth of the jar. Do NOT allow the ice bag to fall in the water.
3. In a few minutes, notice that fog begins forming inside the jar.

Part B:

1. Place several ice cubes inside a perfectly dry metal can.
2. Wait a few minutes; notice that moisture begins forming on the outside of the can.

   Note: Part B of this activity works best when the relative humidity in the room is over 50%.

Explanation

Part A:
The hot water makes the air in the jar warm and moist. The warm, moist air rises toward the top of the jar where it is suddenly cooled by the ice. As the temperature drops, the moisture condenses (goes from a gas to a liquid), making a swirling fog inside the jar.

Part B:
The temperature of the air outside the can is lowered when it comes in contact with the ice-filled can. The water vapor in the air condenses on the outside of the can, forming dew. The temperature at which dew first appears on a surface is called the dew point.

FOLLOW THE BOUNCING BALL

ACTIVITY-AT-A-GLANCE

Purpose

Demonstrates how temperature affects the bounce of a ball.

When to Use

Curricular Area	Difficulty Level	Time to Do

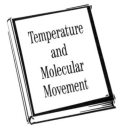

Temperature and Molecular Movement

1 minute
(plus 30 minutes freezing time)

What You'll Need

- ❏ Tennis ball
- ❏ Yardstick
- ❏ Freezer

What to Do

1. Hold the yardstick with one hand and place the ball at the top of its edge.

2. Release the ball and measure the height of the bounce. (Optional: Repeat this step 3 times, and get the average reading.)

3. Place the ball in the freezer for 30 minutes.

4. Repeat Steps 1 and 2.

Explanation

After the ball has been in the freezer, it does not bounce as high because the molecules are moving more slowly due to the cold. The warmer the materials, the faster the molecules will move. The faster the molecules move, the higher the ball will bounce. Playing tennis in cold weather would definitely have an effect on your game.

HI, SWEETY PIE!

ACTIVITY-AT-A-GLANCE

Purpose

Shows that particle size, temperature, and agitation are conditions that affect the rate at which a substance will dissolve in a solution.

When to Use

Curricular Area	Difficulty Level	Time to Do
Temperature; Molecular Movement	4	10 minutes

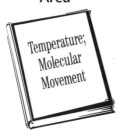

10 minutes

What You'll Need

- ❏ 4 sugar cubes
- ❏ 2 small sheets of paper
- ❏ 2 plastic sandwich bags
- ❏ Felt-tip marker
- ❏ 4 jars, all about the same size
- ❏ Very hot tap water
- ❏ Cold water
- ❏ Several ice cubes
- ❏ 2 plastic spoons

What to Do

1. Wrap 2 sugar cubes in separate pieces of paper.
2. Place each wrapped cube in a separate plastic bag and crush the 2 cubes into powder by stepping on the bags.
3. With a marker, label 2 jars "hot" and 2 jars "cold."
4. Fill the hot jars halfway with hot water.
5. Fill the cold water jars halfway with cold water, then add an ice cube or two to each one.
6. Carefully take the crushed sugar cube out of one bag and pour it into one of the jars of hot water.
7. Quickly drop a whole sugar cube into the other jar of hot water.
8. Stir each container with a spoon and observe.
9. Record how many seconds it takes for the sugar to dissolve.
10. Repeat Steps 6 and 7 with the cold jars of water.

Explanation

The hot water with crushed sugar dissolves much faster than the cold water with the whole cube. Coming in second place is either the cold water/crushed cube or the hot water/whole cube solution. The smaller the particles of a solute (sugar cube), the faster the solute will dissolve. The warmer the temperature of the solvent (water), the faster the solute will dissolve. In other words, when you increase temperature and surface area, you increase the rate of reaction.

JUST HOW BIG IS WATER, ANYWAY?

 ACTIVITY-AT-A-GLANCE

Purpose

Demonstrates the expansion and contraction of water.

When to Use

Curricular Area	Difficulty Level	Time to Do

5 minutes

(plus several hours of cooling and freezing time)

What You'll Need

- ❏ 3 glass baby-food jars
- ❏ Small pan
- ❏ Stove or other heat source
- ❏ Refrigerator with a freezer
- ❏ Small piece of cardboard

What to Do

Part A:

1. Fill one jar to the brim with water.

2. Fill the pan with approximately an inch of water.

3. Heat the jar, gently, in the pan.

4. Notice that the water in the jar overflows.

Part B:

1. Fill another jar to the brim with water.

2. Cool it in the refrigerator for several hours.

3. Notice that the jar is not quite as full.

Part C:

1. Fill the third jar to the brim with water.

2. Cap it with the piece of cardboard.

3. Place the jar in the freezer until water is frozen.

4. Notice that the cardboard is forced off the lip of the jar.

Explanation

A. Water, like other liquids, fills more space when heated. The molecules bounce against one another more rapidly and spread out.

B. Until the temperature of water drops to 39° Fahrenheit, water contracts—takes up less space—as it gets colder. The molecules move more slowly, and closer together.

C. When the temperature of water goes below 39° to its freezing point of 32°, it expands—takes up more room. Water is one of the few chemicals to behave this way.

MOTHBALL FROST

ACTIVITY-AT-A-GLANCE

Purpose

Illustrates how matter can change from a solid to a vapor, then return to a solid.

When to Use

Curricular Area	Difficulty Level	Time to Do

Phase Change; Sublimination

2

10 minutes

What You'll Need

- ❑ 1 mothball
- ❑ A glass jar with a lid
- ❑ Pan
- ❑ Water
- ❑ Stove or other heat source

What to Do

1. Place the mothball in the jar, then place the lid on the jar.
2. Fill the pan with water and place it on the stove.
3. Place the jar in the pan and heat gently until the mothball changes to a vapor.
4. Remove the jar from the heat and allow it to cool. Observe.

 SAFETY NOTE: Avoid touching the mothball during the experiment. Do not inhale the vapors that the mothball gives off.

Explanation

The mothball changed from a solid to an invisible vapor, that is, the mothball got smaller and smaller until it eventually disappeared. This process is called sublimation. The vapor—the distinctive smell of mothballs—is what actually repels moths. When the vaporized mothball was removed from the heat, it cool and changed back to a solid in the form of crystals.

PEPPER IN THE PIE TIN

ACTIVITY-AT-A-GLANCE

Purpose

Shows that cold water molecules move slower than warm water molecules.

When to Use

Curricular Area	Difficulty Level	Time to Do
 Molecular Movement; Heat Energy		 **5 minutes**

What You'll Need

- ❏ 2 pie plates (pie pans or tins)
- ❏ Cup of hot tap water
- ❏ Cup of cold tap water
- ❏ Pepper shaker
- ❏ Liquid soap in a small jar

SkyLight Training and Publishing Inc.

What to Do

1. Fill one pie plate with hot water and the other with cold water.
2. Sprinkle some pepper evenly on the water in each pie plate.
3. Dip the tip of your finger into the liquid soap in the jar.
4. Slowly immerse that finger near the edge of the warm water plate. Observe.
5. Repeat Steps 3 and 4 with the cold water plate.

Explanation

The pepper in the cold water does not "scatter" very far when your soapy finger is placed in the water, while the pepper will definitely "scatter" in the warm water. Molecules of the cold surface have greater density, moving less rapidly than the lighter warm water particles. Note also that the molecular structure of the soap repels the water molecules, breaking the surface tension between the water and the pepper.

PLOP, PLOP, FIZZ, FIZZ

ACTIVITY-AT-A-GLANCE

Purpose

Demonstrates how a reaction rate can be affected by temperature.

When to Use

Curricular Area	Difficulty Level	Time to Do

Chemical Reaction Rates

2

10 minutes

What You'll Need

- ❏ 3 baby-food jars
- ❏ Cold tap water
- ❏ Hot tap water
- ❏ Room-temperature tap water
- ❏ 3 effervescent antacid tablets
- ❏ Clock or watch with a second hand

What to Do

1. Pour cold water in one jar, room temperature water in another jar, and hot water into the third jar.

2. Drop a tablet, at the same time, into each one of the jars.

3. Time how long it takes for each tablet to completely dissolve.

Explanation

The speed at which molecules move depends upon the temperature: the hotter the liquid, the faster the reaction rate or speed of reaction; the colder the liquid, the slower the reaction rate.

Variation

Use a liquid other than water for the activity, record the different times, and chart the results.

POLAR BEAR IN UNDERWEAR

 ## ACTIVITY-AT-A-GLANCE

Purpose

Illustrates how fat acts as an insulator against cold.

When to Use

Curricular Area	Difficulty Level	Time to Do

Temperature and Insulators

5 minutes

What You'll Need

- ❏ 2 quart-size zip-type plastic bags
- ❏ Solid white vegetable shortening
- ❏ Large tray of ice water

What to Do

1. Spread a $\frac{1}{2}$-inch thick layer of the shortening on the inside of one side of the first bag. Try not to get any of the shortening in the zip closure area.
2. Turn the second bag inside out, and put it inside the first bag so that the shortening layer is between the bags.
3. On the nonshortening side of the inside bag, spread another layer of shortening between the two bags.
4. Zip the bags together.
5. Place one of your hands inside this "glove".
6. Place both hands in the tray of ice water.

Explanation

When both hands are placed in the water, the hand with the glove feels very warm because the protective layer of shortening acts as an insulator. This shortening is pure fat and acts as the fat layer under a polar bear's coat does, protecting it from the frigid air and icy arctic waters of the North Pole.

PRESERVING SNOWFLAKES

ACTIVITY-AT-A-GLANCE

Purpose

Illustrates how to collect and preserve snowflake samples for analysis.

When to Use

Curricular Area	Difficulty Level	Time to Do

Crystallization

4

5 minutes
(plus 1 hour chilling time and
1 hour drying time)

What You'll Need

- ❏ Microscope slide or a thin, small piece of glass
- ❏ Pincher-type clothespin
- ❏ Clear lacquer spray (available in craft and hardware stores)
- ❏ Hand lens or magnifying glass
- ❏ A snowy day

What to Do

1. Chill the glass slide outdoors in a protected area for 1 hour.
2. When it starts to snow, attach the clothespin to one end of the slide.
3. Hold the slide by the clothespin so your body heat won't warm the slide.
4. Spray the slide with a thin coat of lacquer. (You may want to slightly chill the spray can so the lacquer will not warm up the slide.)
5. Catch a few snowflakes on your slide.
6. Leave the slide in a very cold, protected place for 1 hour. (Outdoors will work better than your refrigerator because the snow will rapidly melt as you bring it in the house.)
7. Bring in your slide and examine the snowflakes' imprints in the lacquer by using the hand lens.

Explanation

This activity works because the snowflake imprints remain permanent in the non–water-soluble lacquer, that is, after the snowflakes melt and the slide dries.

SWEATY PALMS

 ## ACTIVITY-AT-A-GLANCE

Purpose

Shows how liquids pass through skin pores.

When to Use

| Curricular Area | Difficulty Level | Time to Do |

Health;
Human
Anatomy

1

15 minutes

What You'll Need

- ❏ Clear plastic bag, large enough to cover your hand
- ❏ String
- ❏ A partner

What to Do

1. Place your clean, dry hand in the plastic bag.

2. Have your partner tie a piece of string around your wrist to hold the bag in place. Make sure the string is secure but not too tight around your wrist.

3. Keep the bag on your hand for about 15 minutes and observe. Have your partner remove the bag.

Explanation

Small droplets of water began forming on the inside of the bag. The moisture came from the pores of your skin. Your hand was actually sweating, and the moisture was not able to evaporate because the bag trapped the sweat. Sweating is the human body's cooling system, which is why on a hot day you sweat more than on a cool day.

THE ICEBERG

ACTIVITY-AT-A-GLANCE

Purpose

Demonstrates how an iceberg forms and why it floats.

When to Use

Curricular Area	Difficulty Level	Time to Do

Density

3

5 minutes

(plus overnight freezing time)

What You'll Need

- ❏ 6- to 8-inch balloon
- ❏ Water source (faucet)
- ❏ Funnel
- ❏ Sand and/or fine gravel mixture (about 2 cups)
- ❏ Plastic bag (small enough to fit in the filled balloon)
- ❏ Freezer
- ❏ Scissors
- ❏ Deep bucket

What to Do

1. Fit the balloon over a cold water faucet and fill it about $^3/_4$ full of water.
2. Place the funnel in the mouth of the balloon and add the sand or gravel mixture.
3. Tie the end of the balloon.
4. Place the filled balloon in the plastic bag and leave it in the freezer overnight.
5. Remove the balloon from the bag and carefully cut away the balloon material from the frozen water. You now have an iceberg.
6. Put your iceberg in a deep bucket and observe.

Explanation

You will notice only a small amount of the ice is exposed over the surface of the water. The weight of the sand and gravel is greater than the ice; therefore, it sinks below the water level. Because the entire iceberg is less dense than the surrounding water, it will float.

SECTION FIVE

___

IN LIVING COLOR

One morning, as you dress for school, you notice that your new red jacket does not look the same as it did in the store when you bought it. It's too late to change, so you wear the jacket to school. Your students and colleagues compliment you as they see it. You look at your jacket but the color looks different from the way it did at home! What's going on, you ask yourself. Shouldn't everything look the same when you see it in the light? In this section, you and your students will take a new look at colors and see how they relate to the world around you.

COLOR CREATIONS

ACTIVITY-AT-A-GLANCE

Purpose

Shows how colors are created.

When to Use

Curricular Area	Difficulty Level	Time to Do
 The Nature of Color	1	
		5 minutes

What You'll Need

- ❏ 3 baby-food jars
- ❏ Water
- ❏ Red, yellow, and blue food coloring
- ❏ 3 eyedroppers (medicine droppers)
- ❏ Plastic foam egg carton
- ❏ Paper towels (for cleaning up spills)
- ❏ Gallon-size plastic container

What to Do

1. Fill the baby-food jars $^2/_3$ full of water.

2. Add several drops of red food coloring to the first jar. Add several drops of yellow to the second jar, and several drops of blue to the third jar.

3. Using a different eyedropper for each color, fill one dropper with each color of water and squeeze each color into a separate section of the egg carton.

4. Choose another color and mix it with one of the colors from Step 3.

5. Continue to mix and match by adding colors until the egg carton is full. Observe the color combinations.

6. Experiment even more by dumping all the colors into your empty plastic container.

Explanation

You can create many different color combinations by using the three primary colors of red, blue, and yellow. For example, the following primary colors, when mixed in equal amounts, produce secondary colors as noted: Red + Yellow = Orange; Blue + Yellow = Green; Red + Blue = Purple. (All colors combined = Black.)

Variation

Using water-soluble, different-colored markers, draw designs on a coffee filter. Fold the filter into a cone, design side out. Set the filter into a shallow bowl of water. Watch the colors blend.

FANCY COLORS

 ACTIVITY-AT-A-GLANCE

Purpose

Demonstrates how colors are affected by differences in density.

When to Use

Curricular Area	Difficulty Level	Time to Do
 Density	**2**	 **10 minutes**

What You'll Need

- ❏ Clear glass bowl
- ❏ Water
- ❏ Cup
- ❏ Tablespoon of cooking oil
- ❏ Red, blue, and green food coloring
- ❏ Fork

What to Do

1. Fill the bowl ³/₄ full of water.
2. Place the oil in the cup and add 4 drops each of red, blue, and green food coloring.
3. Use the fork to mix the oil and colors thoroughly.
4. Pour the oil and food coloring mixture into the water in the bowl.
5. Observe the action on the surface of the water.

Explanation

The colors appear to explode outward producing circles of color on the water with color streams that sink downward. Oil and water have different densities and do not mix well. Food coloring is water-based, so it is isolated in tiny spheres throughout the oil. The colored spheres sink down through the oil layer and eventually dissolve in the water below.

FLOWER CHILD

 ## ACTIVITY-AT-A-GLANCE

Purpose

Demonstrates the process of plant nourishment.

When to Use

Curricular Area	Difficulty Level	Time to Do

Plant Botany

5 minutes
(plus several hours waiting time)

What You'll Need

- ❏ 4 clear glasses
- ❏ Water
- ❏ 4 different colors of food coloring
- ❏ 4 fresh white carnations, with stems
- ❏ Scissors
- ❏ Warm room

What to Do

1. Pour about 2 inches of water into each glass.
2. Add 2 to 3 drops of each of the different food coloring to each of the glasses.
3. With your scissors, trim the carnation stems so the flowers are 2 inches taller than the glasses.
4. Cut along the stem of each carnation, making a 2-inch incision (lengthwise) in the stem.
5. Place each flower in a different glass of colored water.
6. Leave the flowers in a warm room for a few hours, then observe the results.

Explanation

Each white carnation turned the same color as the food coloring. Tiny veinlike tubes in the flower stem carried the tinted water to the petals of the carnation. This activity demonstrates how plants receive nourishment through these processes known as diffusion and osmosis.

GREEN GOBBLEDYGOOK

ACTIVITY-AT-A-GLANCE

Purpose

Demonstrates the chemical properties of a metal.

When to Use

Curricular Area	Difficulty Level	Time to Do

Chemistry; Chemical Reactions

1

1 minute
(plus 1 day waiting time)

What You'll Need

- ❑ Paper towel
- ❑ Bowl
- ❑ Vinegar (acetic acid)
- ❑ 3 to 5 pennies

SkyLight Training and Publishing Inc.

What to Do

1. Fold a paper towel in quarters.
2. Place the folded towel in the bowl.
3. Pour enough vinegar into the bowl to wet the towel.
4. Place the pennies on top of the wet towel.
5. Wait 24 hours.

Explanation

After the 24 hours have elapsed, the tops of the pennies have turned green. The acetate part of the acid combines with the copper on the pennies to form the green coating, a compound called copper acetate. Color change is one of several indicators that a chemical change has taken place.

I'M SEEING RED NOW

ACTIVITY-AT-A-GLANCE

Purpose

Shows a chemical reaction between an acid and a base.

When to Use

Curricular Area	Difficulty Level	Time to Do
Acid and Base Reactions		 5 minutes

What You'll Need

❏ Cup and tablespoon
❏ Turmeric (available in the spice section of supermarkets)
❏ Rubbing alcohol
❏ Spray bottle of ammonia-based glass cleaner
❏ Paper towel
❏ Small paintbrush

What to Do

1. In the clean cup, add 1 tablespoon of turmeric (in its dry powder form) to 4 ounces of rubbing alcohol. Stir thoroughly.

2. Dipping a brush in this mixture, print a message on the paper towel. Allow your message to dry for a couple of seconds.

3. Hold the towel in one hand and the spray bottle in the other hand. Gently spray the towel until you can read your message.

 SAFETY NOTE: Use caution when spraying the glass cleaner near anyone. Also note that turmeric will stain clothing. Do this activity over a garbage can or container to catch the dripping liquid. Finally, avoid inhaling alcohol fumes.

Explanation

Turmeric is a mild chemical acid. As a finely ground powder, the turmeric dissolves in the alcohol. The glass cleaner contains ammonia, which is a chemical base. As this base hits the acid that has been applied to the paper towel, a vivid red color appears. The root of the tumeric plant has been used for hundreds of years for dyeing as well as for seasoning food. It is also used in chemistry to make test papers for bases (alkalies), a purpose that this experiment demonstrates.

RAINBOW BRIGHT

 ACTIVITY-AT-A-GLANCE

Purpose

Demonstrates the presence of colors in sunlight.

When to Use

Curricular Area	Difficulty Level	Time to Do

Temperature; Molecular Movement

1

2 minutes

What You'll Need

❑ Clear bowl
❑ Water
❑ Small hand mirror
❑ Sunshine

What to Do

1. Fill the clear bowl with water
2. Set the bowl next to a window in direct sunlight.
3. Place the hand mirror in the water.
4. Angle the mirror until the sun is reflected and the colors (like those of a rainbow) shine on a nearby object.

Explanation

Light is made of up of many colors, and when light passes at an angle from air to water (both being transparent), the light separates into a color spectrum. Sometimes after a rainstorm, there is still a lot of water in the air and a rainbow forms as the sun comes out and shines through the mist.

SOMEWHERE OVER THE RAINBOW

 ACTIVITY-AT-A-GLANCE

Purpose

Demonstrates the force of adhesion.

When to Use

Curricular Area	Difficulty Level	Time to Do

Force of Adhesion

15 minutes

What You'll Need

- ❏ Vegetable oil
- ❏ Flat, aluminum pie tin
- ❏ Water
- ❏ Several straws
- ❏ Several colors of oil-based paint
- ❏ Pencil
- ❏ Masking tape
- ❏ Index card or piece of paper

What to Do

1. Lightly oil the inside surface of the aluminum pie tin.

2. Fill the tin with about $1/2$ inch of water.

3. Pick up a small amount of paint with a straw by dipping the end of the straw into the paint, keeping a finger over the other end of the straw. Lift the finger when the straw is above the water.

4. Place 2 drops of the paint on the water.

5. Gently stir the paint into any shape with the pencil point.

6. Use a different straw for each of the paints, add dots of color to the tin of water.

7. Swirl each color as you add the paint or gently blow through the straw for a different effect. (Do not inhale through the straw.)

8. Fasten masking tape loops about 1 to 2 inches in diameter to the back of the index card or piece of paper.

9. Lift the card by the loops and gently place it down on the water.

10. Wait 3 seconds and pick the card up by the loops.

11. Let the card dry.

Explanation

The colors of your paint were attracted to the card or paper due to the force of adhesion. Adhesion is the active force that works when two different substances are brought in contact with one another. The paint remains on the surface of the water because it is oil-based and oil is less dense than water.

SPINNING COLOR DISK

ACTIVITY-AT-A-GLANCE

Purpose

Visualizes the nature of color.

When to Use

Curricular Area	Difficulty Level	Time to Do

Color, Optics

15 minutes

What You'll Need

Part A:
- ❏ Cardboard
- ❏ Piece of white unlined paper
- ❏ Black marker, drawing compass, scissors, glue stick, ruler, black pen

Part B:
- ❏ 3- to 5-inch piece of a two-by-four (or similar size piece of wood)
- ❏ Long finishing nail (long enough to protrude through the wood)
- ❏ Hammer

What to Do

Part A:

1. Using a compass, draw a circle with a 4-inch diameter on the cardboard. NOTE: That would be the 2-inch mark on the compass itself.

2. Cut out the cardboard circle.

3. Using the sharp end of the compass or a pencil point, punch a small hole in the center of the cardboard.

4. Glue your cardboard circle or wheel on top of the white unlined paper.

5. Cut the paper to the size of the wheel.

6. Using the ruler and black pen, divide the paper side of the wheel into 8 even sections.

7. With the black marker, draw different designs and shapes in these sections.

Part B:

1. Pound the nail in the center of the wood. The nail should protrude from the back of the wood at least $3/4$ inch or more.

2. Put the nail through the hole in your wheel.

3. Spin the circle around a few times and vary the speed.

4. Stare directly at the wheel as you spin it.

 SAFETY NOTE: Be careful that no one is injured with the protuding end of the nail.

Explanation

The white spaces on the wheel or disk reflect all of the colors of the rainbow. Each white space is only seen for a short amount of time because it is followed by a black space. With these varying lengths of black and white, the eye (the brain) will perceive only certain colors. When the disk slows down, you can see more of the colors because you have more time to see the white spaces.

A CRYSTAL GARDEN

ACTIVITY-AT-A-GLANCE

Purpose

Demonstrates the processes of evaporation and crystallization

When to Use

Curricular Area	Difficulty Level	Time to Do

Crystal Formation; Evaporation	4	**10 minutes** (plus 1 day of waiting time)

What You'll Need

- ❏ Pie pan (pie plate or tin)
- ❏ 8 to 10 pieces of charcoal briquets **(Note: Do not use charcoal that is treated with lighter fluid.)**
- ❏ 2 to 4 tablespoons each of water, salt, and bluing (available in the soap/laundry section of most supermarkets)
- ❏ 2 tablespoons of ammonia
- ❏ Mixing bowl
- ❏ Food coloring, various colors

SkyLight Training and Publishing Inc.

What to Do

1. Cover the bottom of the pie pan with the charcoal.
2. Mix the water, salt, bluing, and ammonia together in the mixing bowl.
3. Carefully pour the mixture over the charcoal. Make sure all the charcoal pieces get wet.
4. Squirt a few drops of food coloring, various colors in random order, on the charcoal.
5. Set the pie pan aside in an undisturbed, airy place for one day.
6. Observe the colorful, flowerlike growth (the crystallization) that occurs.

 SAFETY NOTE: If you tell your students to experiment with a different variables in this activity, caution them never to use bleach with ammonia, as the reaction will produce poisonous gases.

Explanation

The salt crystal garden is formed by the recrystallizing of the salt. As the water evaporates, including the water in the bluing (a colloidal suspension of iron, carbon, and nitrogen molecules), the blue particles can no longer be supported and the excess salt dries out. The salt crystallizes around the bluing particles. The ammonia starts to break down the charcoal into a liquid, aiding the evaporation process. The remaining charcoal soaks up the additional moisture until it is completely saturated. As the liquid evaporates, the salt solution begins to dry and recrystallizes in new forms.

Variation

Other porous materials can be used as the base of the garden, such as a piece of porous brick or a sponge.

EVERYDAY ACIDS AND BASES

ACTIVITY-AT-A-GLANCE

Purpose

Shows that materials commonly found in the kitchen are acids or bases.

When to Use

Curricular Area	Difficulty Level	Time to Do
 Acids and Bases; pH Factor		 15 minutes

What You'll Need

- ❏ Hot water
- ❏ Small amounts of natural indicators: red cabbage, red apple skin, cherries, beets, and grape juice
- ❏ Knife (to chop up natural indicators)
- ❏ 12 or more small jars
- ❏ Strainer

- ❏ 1 tablespoon each of these common acids: lemon juice, orange juice, vitamin C tablets (pulverized), soda pop, and vinegar
- ❏ 1 tablespoon each of these common bases: baking soda, liquid antacid, ammonia (or ammonia-based glass cleaner), and egg white

What to Do

1. Using your knife, prepare the natural indicators by chopping the materials into small bits, then pour hot water over them. Strain off the solid material and store each indicator solution in its own jar. The solid material can later be diluted, using equal parts of water, to create more liquid indicators.
2. In each of the jars, place 1 tablespoon of one of the indicator solutions. The first jar should be your control (use for color comparison). Add nothing to this jar.
3. Add 1 tablespoon of lemon juice to the second jar. Add other acids to the other jars, keeping track of the color changes.
4. Repeat Step 3 with the common bases.
5. Repeat Steps 3 and 4 with other natural indicators.

Explanation

The color changes are chemical reactions. Indicators show pH level, that is how acidic or basic a material is. When using the cabbage indicator in this activity, for instance, note that a resulting pink color range indicates acidic quality; a blue/green/violet color range indicates a basic quality. pH levels range from 1 (strong acid) to 14 (strong base).

Variation

Have students work with pH test paperstrips or litmus paper, available in science supply stores or drugstores, to extend their experience with pH level testing.

THE COLOR OF BLACK

ACTIVITY-AT-A-GLANCE

Purpose

Demonstrates chromatography.

When to Use

Curricular Area	Difficulty Level	Time to Do
 Chemistry; Chromatography	3	 15 minutes

What You'll Need

- ❏ Coffee filters or paper towels
- ❏ Cup
- ❏ Scissors
- ❏ Water-soluble, black felt-tip marker
- ❏ Water

What to Do

1. Using the coffee filters or paper towels, cut strips about 1-inch wide and about 1 to 2 inches longer than the depth of the cup.

2. With your marker, draw a horizontal line across the strip about 1 inch from the bottom.

3. Fill the cup with about 1 inch of water.

4. Place the strip in the water so that the bottom of the strip just touches the water. The ink line must be above the water level. You may bend the top of the strip over the edge of the cup.

5. Observe the movement of the water and color until the color band spreads up the strip of paper. This should take about 5 to 10 minutes.

6. Remove the strip and allow it to dry.

Explanation

This experiment demonstrates chromatography, a process by which the components of a liquid are absorbed by paper at different rates. The liquid begins to move the components of the ink outward at different rates of speed along the porous paper. These molecules interact less strongly with the paper and more strongly with the liquid being drawn up into the paper with the moving liquid. The result is that the colors that make up the ink separate into different color bands. The movement of liquid through paper in this activity is an example of capillary action.

Variation

Try using different types of papers and different colors of water-soluble felt-tip markers.

SECTION SIX

———

STATIC IN THE ATTIC

Remember the last time the electricity went out—when there was a power outage due to a storm or other problem? Discuss with your students what you (and they) did for light when it got dark. How did you all get by? Have students reflect on the fact that the longer the power outage lasted, the more likely it was to have a serious effect—such as accidents resulting from traffic lights that were out. When the power returned and the lights went back on, you all breathed a sign of relief, didn't you? In the activities in this section, you and your students will take a fresh look at electricity and light.

A LOOK THROUGH A LENS

 ACTIVITY-AT-A-GLANCE

Purpose

Shows how a convex lens works to magnify.

When to Use

Curricular Area	Difficulty Level	Time to Do

Optics;
Magnification

1 minute

What You'll Need

❑ A clear plastic glass
❑ Water

SkyLight Training and Publishing Inc.

What to Do

1. Fill the glass with water.
2. Hold one finger behind the glass.
3. Look closely at that finger through the glass.

Explanation

Your finger looks larger than it actually is because the glass of water is curved the same way as a convex lens. Both the curved glass of water and a convex lens bend light to make an image appear larger. If you cannot see objects up close, you use a convex lens to make the objects larger. Different types of lenses are used in magnifying glasses, telescopes, microscopes, and eyeglasses/bifocals.

Variation

The opposite of convex is concave. To demonstrate an example of a concave lens, hold the eyeglasses of a person who is nearsighted (or cannot see objects well from a distance) a few inches above a page of newsprint. The print will actually look smaller.

BOUNCE THAT OFF ME

ACTIVITY-AT-A-GLANCE

Purpose

Simulates the path that light takes when it hits a curved reflector.

When to Use

Curricular Area	Difficulty Level	Do

Light: Optics, and Reflection

4 minutes

What You'll Need

- ❏ 4-foot section of plastic tubing about ¹/₂-inch in diameter (available in hardware stores)
- ❏ Tape
- ❏ 2- to 3-inch rubber ball
- ❏ Tabletop

What to Do

1. Tape the tubing in a semicircular curve upright on the tabletop.

2. Starting from about a foot back, start the ball rolling toward the top of the tubing. Notice the angle at which the ball bounces off the tube.

3. Now roll the ball from the opposite side of the tube. Notice the angle that it bounces off the tubing. (Note: The point at which the two balls cross is called the focal point.)

4. Continue rolling the ball toward various points on the tube and you should notice that the ball always bounces toward the center area (the focal point).

Explanation

A curved mirror, which the semicircular tube represents, is like a series of flat mirrors. Each flat mirror is tilted slightly to give a curved effect. When light strikes any point on the mirror, it is as if it were hitting a flat mirror. The light is reflected at the same angle at which it hits the reflector, as the ball in this experiment is "reflected" off the tubing at the same angle. The effect of the curve is to reflect all the light rays to a single point, called the focal point. If you were to place a light at the focal point of a curved mirror, then the rays of light would reflect off the mirror and form a beam of light. This is how a flashlight, headlight, or spotlight works.

Variation

Place a sheet of paper under the tubing and use a pencil to record the path of the ball. This way you can mark exactly where the focal point is located.

COMPASS MAGIC

 ACTIVITY-AT-A-GLANCE

Purpose

Demonstrates how to make a compass.

When to Use

Curricular Area	Difficulty Level	Time to Do
Magnetism: Use of a Compass		 15 minutes

What You'll Need

- ❏ Plastic dish half-filled with water
- ❏ Sewing needle
- ❏ Straight pin
- ❏ Bar magnet
- ❏ Clear tape
- ❏ Small piece of wood
- ❏ Sheet of paper

SkyLight Training and Publishing Inc.

What to Do

1. Center the dish of water on the paper.
2. Hold the needle by the thick end and rub it from one end of the magnet to the other about 12 times in the same direction.
3. Test the needle to see if it picks up the straight pin. If not, rub the needle on the magnet a few more times.
4. Tape the needle onto the wood and place it in the water.
5. Watch the needle until it stops turning.
6. Mark the direction of the needle point on the paper. (It should be pointing north.)

Explanation

Rubbing a needle with a magnet creates a magnetic field because the magnetic domains (groups of molecules) within the needle become aligned, the north poles facing one direction and the south poles facing the other direction. The needle becomes magnetized and turns into a compass always pointing north when it is free to turn.

Variation

Try this experiment with different types of materials. Compare the results. You will discover that only objects attracted by a magnet can be magnetized.

STUCK-UP PARSLEY

 ACTIVITY-AT-A-GLANCE

Purpose

Illustrates how static electricity can be created.

When to Use

Curricular Area	Difficulty Level	Time to Do

Static Electricity

1

5 minutes

What You'll Need

- ❏ Parsley (dried flakes)
- ❏ Plastic foam cup
- ❏ Wool or silk (optional)

SkyLight Training and Publishing Inc.

What to Do

1. Place a pinch of parsley in the cup.
2. Rub the cup against your hair, arm, a piece of silk, or wool for 30 seconds.
3. Look inside the cup.

   Note: This activity works best when the relative humidity in the air is under 50%.

Explanation

Static electricity is a buildup of negatively charges electrons looking for a place to go. The charges build up, usually on cool, dry days, and when contact is made (such as your feet walking across a carpet)—ZAP! The excess charges have to go somewhere, so they give you a mild electric shock as they jump.

Variation

Try this activity using other foods, such as unflavored gelatin. Also try using other containers such as plastic plates. Can you pick up any of the food items with a charged-up balloon?

DON'T GET ALL PUFFY ON ME

 ACTIVITY-AT-A-GLANCE

Purpose

Illustrates the effect of static electricity.

When to Use

Curricular Area	Difficulty Level	Time to Do

Static Electricity

3 minutes

What You'll Need

- ❏ Hard rubber or nylon comb
- ❏ Container of warm, soapy water
- ❏ Piece of puffed rice (cereal)
- ❏ 2 feet of sewing thread
- ❏ Piece of wool cloth
- ❏ Table
- ❏ Adhesive tape

SkyLight Training and Publishing Inc.

What to Do

1. Wash the comb in the soapy water to remove any oil or dirt that may be on it.
2. Tie one end of the thread to the puffed rice.
3. Tape the free end to the center of the table. The cereal should be able to move freely without touching any other object.
4. Rub the length of the comb along the wool cloth about 15 to 20 strokes.
5. Carefully bring the comb near the end of the suspended piece of puffed rice. Do not touch it. The comb should be about $1/2$ inch from the puffed rice.

   Note: This activity works best when the relative humidity of the air is under 50%.

Explanation

The piece of puffed rice is pulled toward the comb. When you rubbed the comb, it built up negative charges of electricity, which the comb picked up from the wool cloth. The puffed rice built up negative charges when it touched the comb. Static electricity is a buildup of negatively charged electrons looking for a place to go. Since like charges (– and –) repel each other, the two objects pushed apart.

Variation

Try other small objects to tie onto the thread. See if you are able to charge up some other type of object other than a comb.

EXTRA, EXTRA, READ ALL ABOUT IT!

ACTIVITY-AT-A-GLANCE

Purpose

Shows how friction causes static electricity.

When to Use

Curricular Area	Difficulty Level	Time to Do

Frictional Forces; Static Electricity

1 minute

What You'll Need

- ❏ Small, smooth page of newsprint (from a newspaper)
- ❏ Pencil
- ❏ Smooth wall

What to Do

1. Hold a page of newsprint to the wall with one hand.
2. Quickly stroke the page with the side of the pencil about 20 times.
3. Move back and observe the paper.
4. Peel up one corner, and let it go.

   Note: This activity works best when the relative humidity of the air is under 50%.

Explanation

The paper stuck to the wall. When you peeled it back, it quickly returned to the wall. The friction between the pencil and the paper developed an electrical charge in the paper. This static electrical charge caused the paper to be attracted to the wall.

THE BOUNCING LIGHT

ACTIVITY-AT-A-GLANCE

Purpose

Demonstrates that light travels in straight lines, which can be directed by mirrors.

When to Use

Curricular Area	Difficulty Level	Time to Do
 Optics and Reflection	4	 5 minutes

What You'll Need

- ❏ Two 8-inch squares of cardboard
- ❏ Nail
- ❏ Clay
- ❏ Flashlight
- ❏ 2 cardboard paper towel tubes
- ❏ Dark room
- ❏ Mirror

What to Do

Part A:

1. Poke a hole with the nail through the center of both pieces of cardboard.
2. Break up the clay into several small chunks.
3. Line up the cardboard pieces about 12 inches apart, one behind the other.
4. Place the flashlight at one end of the cardboard and shine it through both of the holes.
5. Now slowly turn the second cardboard sideways, as you shine the beam of light through the holes. Observe.

Part B:

1. Set up the two paper towel tubes at angles near the mirror.
2. Shine the flashlight at one end of a tube to bounce light off the mirror and through the second tube.
3. You may need the help of an assistant here. Direct the light from the second tube to any object in the room.

Explanation

Light will travel in a straight line unless there is something that acts as interference to the light beam. Also, light rays can be reflected and redirected.

DON'T TAKE IT SO LIGHTLY

ACTIVITY-AT-A-GLANCE

Purpose

Shows how interference affects magnetic forces.

When to Use

Curricular Area	Difficulty Level	Time to Do
Magnetism	3	 5 minutes

What You'll Need

- ❏ Several thick books (enough to make a 10-inch stack)
- ❏ 15 inches of string
- ❏ Large paper clip
- ❏ 12-inch ruler
- ❏ Bar magnet
- ❏ Small nail, piece of paper, cardboard, cloth, and plastic wrap

What to Do

1. Stack the books.
2. Tie one end of the sting to the paper clip.
3. Place the magnet on top of the books with one end (one "pole") extending a few inches over the edge of the stack of books.
4. Fasten the string to the ruler.
5. Place the ruler under the magnet and suspend the paper clip so it is about 1 inch from the magnet. The clip should "levitate" due to the magnetic force of the bar magnet.
6. Without touching the clip or the magnet, slowly move the piece of paper between the magnet and the clip.
7. Repeat with the other objects. Each time the clip falls, carefully suspend it again.

Explanation

Not all objects are magnetic. Objects that are magnetic will cause the paper clip to fall. Those objects that are not magnetic can pass between a magnet and a magnetic object without interfering with the force.

Variation

Run different objects through your magnet paper clip device.

LOSING MONEY

 ACTIVITY-AT-A-GLANCE

Purpose

Illustrates how light reflection can create an optical illusion.

When to Use

Curricular Area	Difficulty Level	Time to Do

Reflection; Optical Illusion	1	1 minute

What You'll Need

- ❏ Large, deep bowl
- ❏ Water
- ❏ Clear drinking glass
- ❏ Coin

What to Do

1. Fill the bowl nearly to the top with water.
2. Place a coin in the center of the bowl.
3. Invert the glass and carefully place it over the coin. Do not allow water to flow into the glass.
4. Look through the side of the glass and try to find the coin.

Explanation

The coin seemed to disappear because, from most angles of observation, the light rays were totally reflected at the boundary between the water and the glass. So these light rays did not bounce back and reach your eye.

MAY THE FORCE BE WITH YOU

ACTIVITY-AT-A-GLANCE

Purpose

Identifies materials through which a magnetic force will pass.

When to Use

Curricular Area	Difficulty Level	Time to Do

5 minutes

What You'll Need

- ❏ A few $1\frac{1}{4}$-inch paper clips
- ❏ Various materials such as thin pieces of paper, wood, glass, leather, and construction paper
- ❏ U-shaped magnet
- ❏ Small wide-mouthed jar filled with water

What to Do

1. Place a couple of paper clips on top of the different materials to be tested.
2. Place the magnet underneath the materials.
3. Move the magnet slowly to see if the paper clips follow the magnet.
4. Next, place the paper clips in the water-filled jar, hold the magnet just over the surface of the water, and observe.

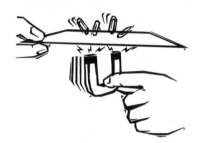

Explanation

The magnetic force will pass through any of the materials, depending on several factors: the thickness of the solid material, the strength of the magnet, and the distance between the magnet and the solid. Magnetism will also work through water, as it is used in step 4.

Variation

Try step 4 using liquids of different viscosity, such as milk or syrup instead of water. Observe how the magnetic force is affected.

PARTLY CLOUDY

 ACTIVITY-AT-A-GLANCE

Purpose

Demonstrates condensation and how clouds can be observed in the dark.

When to Use

Curricular Area	Difficulty Level	Time to Do

Condensation; Cloud Formation

5 minutes

What You'll Need

- ❏ Hot water (from the tap)
- ❏ Glass jar with a lid
- ❏ Several ice cubes
- ❏ Plastic bag
- ❏ Chalk dust
- ❏ Flashlight

What to Do

1. Fill the jar halfway with hot water.
2. Place the lid, upside-down, on top of the jar.
3. Place the ice cubes in the plastic bag.
4. Blow some chalk dust into the jar.
5. Place the ice-filled bag on top of the lid.
6. Turn off the lights in the room, making it as dark as possible.
7. Shine the flashlight through the jar and observe the condensation process.

Explanation

A cloud formed when the warm air from the jar came in contact with the cold air. The chalk dust provided particles to which the droplets could stick. The flashlight used in the darkened room made it easier to observe the condensation process.

YOU LIGHT UP MY LIFE

 ACTIVITY-AT-A-GLANCE

Purpose

Demonstrates how light is produced by static electricity.

When to Use

Curricular Area	Difficulty Level	Time to Do

Static Electricity, Friction

2

1 minute

What You'll Need

❑ One 2-foot fluorescent light tube
❑ Piece of wool material

What to Do

1. In a totally darkened room, hold the fluorescent light tube at one end.
2. Using the wool cloth, vigorously rub the tube along its length.

   Note that this activity works best when the relative humidity of the air is under 50%.

 SAFETY NOTE: Teacher demonstration only. Use extreme caution when rubbing the tube with the cloth. Do not apply excess pressure on the glass tube; it might break in your hands. Wear a thick pair of gloves and safety glasses in case the glass shatters. Advise students to keep at a safe distance.

Explanation

The friction between the wool and the glass caused the negatively charged electrons to strike and dislodge from the atoms in the gas inside the tube. As these dislodged electrons tried to get back to their original atoms, they gave off their energy in the form of light and the tube gave off light accordingly.

SECTION SEVEN

AiR AND WATER PRESSURE

Most everyone is familiar with the word *pressure,* but perhaps the first thing that comes to mind is, let's say, pressure that you feel as a teacher or pressure your students feel to get good grades. In this section, you and your students will look at pressure from a scientific perspective. The activities in this section are focused on air and water pressure, which can be measured and observed. Younger students may not think of air and water having pressure, but after this section, you will have them convinced. The pressure in on!

TRY YOUR STRENGTH!

 ACTIVITY-AT-A-GLANCE

Purpose

Illustrates the formation of a change in air pressure.

When to Use

Curricular Area	Difficulty Level	Time to Do

Air Pressure

1 minute

What You'll Need

- ❑ Wide-mouthed glass jar
- ❑ Plastic sandwich bag
- ❑ Rubberband

What to Do

Part 1:

1. Place the bag opening over the mouth of the jar.
2. Use the rubberband to tightly hold the bag in place.
3. Try to push the bag into the jar.

Part 2:

1. Remove the rubberband from Part 1.
2. Place the bag inside the jar.
3. Use the rubberband to tightly fasten the bag around the mouth of the jar.
4. Try to pull the bag out of the jar.

Explanation

Part 1: When you pressed on the bag, the volume of air in the jar was trapped. The trapped air had no where to go and formed a resistance that made it difficult for you to push the bag into the jar.

Part 2: When the bag was already in the jar and you attempted to pull it out, the pressure decreased inside the jar, thus making the outside air pressure much greater.

BLAST OFF

ACTIVITY-AT-A-GLANCE

Purpose

Illustrates the principle of rocket engines.

When to Use

Curricular Area	Difficulty Level	Time to Do

Jet Propulsion

5 minutes

What You'll Need

- ❏ 2-liter plastic soda bottle
- ❏ Rubber stopper (must be able to fit halfway into the soda bottle)
- ❏ Air pump (such as one for inflating balls or bicycle tires)
- ❏ Needle for such a pump
- ❏ Ice pick
- ❏ Water

What to Do

1. Place 1 cup of water into the bottle.
2. Using the ice pick, carefully make a hole in the center of the rubber stopper to allow the needle to be inserted.
3. Attach the needle to the pump.
4. Place the stopper snugly into the bottle. *Do not force it in.*
5. Place the bottle on its side. Aim the bottle into an open area outside and begin to pump air into the bottle. Do NOT pause as you pump or the water will back up into the pump.

 SAFETY NOTE: Teacher activity only, or at least adult-monitored. Do not do this activity indoors. Do not stand in front of the bottle as it is being filled with air. Caution observers to stand at a safe distance.

Explanation

As air is pumped into the bottle, the pressure inside the bottle increased. As the pressure continued to increase inside the bottle, the stopper was pushed out, which caused the air and water inside the bottle to rush out; this creates a rocket-engine effect. Your bottle launched with a powerful WHOOSH!

IT WON'T FILL UP!

 ACTIVITY-AT-A-GLANCE

Purpose

Demonstrates how lack of pressure affects gravity.

When to Use

Curricular Area	Difficulty Level	Time to Do

Air Pressure

2 minutes

What You'll Need

- ❏ Funnel
- ❏ Empty soda bottle
- ❏ Small piece of clay
- ❏ Water

What to Do

1. Place the funnel in the neck of the empty soda bottle.
2. Place clay around the neck of the bottle so that there is no space between the funnel and the bottle.
3. Pour water in the funnel and observe.
4. Remove the clay and observe.

Explanation

While the clay is on the neck of the bottle, the water remains in the funnel or enters in slow spurts. The clay forms a seal in which the air cannot escape, except by going through the water very slowly. The air in the bottle takes up space and prevents the water from coming in. This seems to defy gravity, but it is simply a matter of air pressure. When the clay is removed and the air is able to escape around the neck of the bottle, the water can flow into the bottle, which proves that air takes up space and has pressure.

BOTTLE
FOUNTAIN

 ACTIVITY-AT-A-GLANCE

Purpose

Demonstrates how temperature change affects water pressure.

When to Use

Curricular Area	Difficulty Level	Time to Do

Water Pressure; Temperature

10 minutes

What You'll Need

❏ 12- or 16-ounce plastic soda bottle with screw-top cap
❏ Nail or sharp instrument
❏ Clear drinking straw
❏ Silicone sealant, plasticine sealant, caulk, or other sealing material
❏ Ice-cold water
❏ Very hot tap water
❏ Large bowl

What to Do

1. Carefully punch or cut a hole in the top of the bottle cap, making it large enough for the drinking straw to pass through it.

2. Screw the cap on the bottle.

3. Push the straw through the hole about halfway.

4. Seal the gap between the screw cap and the straw with the sealant. This seal has to be airtight. You may have to allow the sealant to dry before you proceed, depending on the type of sealant you use.

5. Carefully remove the cap and fill the bottle with the ice-cold water.

6. Screw the cap on the bottle very tightly.

7. Fill the bowl with very hot water.

8. Place the bottle in the bowl and observe.

 SAFETY NOTE: Use caution when punching or cutting a hole in the bottle cap.

Explanation

The water started to shoot out of the straw like a fountain. When the cold water was placed in the bottle, it cooled the surrounding air molecules. The hot water then heated up those molecules and caused the air to expand. The expanding air pressed down on the water and forced the water out of the straw.

DING DONG DIVER

ACTIVITY-AT-A-GLANCE

Purpose

Illustrates the nature of fluid pressure.

When to Use

Curricular Area	Difficulty Level	Time to Do
 Fluid Pressure; Mass	2	 1 minute

What You'll Need

- ❏ 1 liter- or smaller-size plastic soda bottle
- ❏ Eyedropper
- ❏ Water

What to Do

1. Fill the bottle to the very top with water.
2. Fill the eyedropper about half-full with water.
3. Place the dropper in the soda bottle. The dropper should be standing upright in the bottle. (If not, take the eyedropper out and add more water. Replace eyedropper.)
4. Cap the bottle.
5. Squeeze the bottle firmly with both hands and observe the result.

Explanation

When you squeezed the bottle, the dropper fell down to the bottom of the bottle because you forced water into the dropper, increasing its mass. When you released the bottle, the dropper returned to its original position (standing upright) because you decreased the water pressure on the dropper. The water was expelled from the dropper and was replaced with air. Thus, the mass became less and the dropper rose accordingly. This activity is often called the "Cartesian Diver" and is a classic science experiment.

FLY AWAY

 ACTIVITY-AT-A-GLANCE

Purpose

Illustrates movement of air due to unequal pressure.

When to Use

Curricular Area	Difficulty Level	Time to Do
 Air Pressure	1	 1 minute

What You'll Need

❏ Empty, narrow-necked soda bottle
❏ Small piece of paper (1-inch x 1-inch square)

What to Do

1. Lay the soda bottle on its side.

2. Crumple the paper into a small wad and place it just inside the mouth of the bottle. The wad should fit loosely.

3. Try to blow the paper wad into the bottle with your breath.

Explanation

Before you blow into the bottle, the amount of air inside and outside the bottle is the same. The extra air blown into the bottle increases the air pressure inside. This extra air is pushed out of the opening, and the moving air swishes the paper wad out of the bottle.

GENIE IN THE BOTTLE

ACTIVITY-AT-A-GLANCE

Purpose

Exhibits the change in air volume caused by temperature change.

When to Use

Curricular Area	Difficulty Level	Time to Do

Vacuum Formation; Air Pressure

5 minutes

What You'll Need

- ❏ Hot plate, stove, or other heat source
- ❏ Pot
- ❏ Water
- ❏ Funnel
- ❏ Oven mitt
- ❏ 2- or 3-liter plastic pop bottle (label removed)
- ❏ Bowl full of ice-cold water

SkyLight Training and Publishing Inc.

What to Do

1. Boil about 1 cup of water in the pot.
2. Using the funnel, carefully pour the hot water into the plastic bottle.
3. Wearing the mitt, turn the bottle back and forth so the water swishes around in the bottle for a couple of minutes, heating up the air in the bottle.
4. Empty the hot water from the bottle and immediately invert the bottle over the bowl of ice-cold water, keeping the neck of the bottle slightly under the surface of the water at all times.
5. Hold the bottle in place for a minute or so and observe that the water rises several inches into the plastic bottle.

 SAFETY NOTE: Teacher activity only. Use caution when pouring the hot water into the bottle. Avoid spilling the water out of the bottle in Step 3.

Explanation

When the heated air in the bottle cooled, a vacuum was formed, since cool air takes up less space than hot air. The water was pushed into the bottle by the pressure of the surrounding air.

Variation

You may tint the water with food coloring for a special effect.

HUFF 'N' PUFF

 ACTIVITY-AT-A-GLANCE

Purpose

Demonstrates that air takes up space.

When to Use

Curricular Area	Difficulty Level	Time to Do
Properties of Air and Matter		 1 minute

What You'll Need

❏ Balloon
❏ Empty glass soda bottle

What to Do

1. Push the deflated balloon into the bottle and stretch the open end back over the bottle's mouth.

2. Blow into the balloon as hard as you can.

Explanation

As you inflate the balloon, it takes up additional space in the bottle. But the bottle is already full of air before you begin. Even though you cannot see it, this air takes up space. When you try to blow up the balloon, the air trapped inside the bottle prevents you from doing it.

NO JOKING MATTER

ACTIVITY-AT-A-GLANCE

Purpose

Demonstrates how an emulsion can be used to copy print from a newspaper.

When to Use

Curricular Area	Difficulty Level	Time to Do
 Mixtures/ Solutions		 **5 minutes**

What You'll Need

- ❑ 4 tablespoons of water
- ❑ 2 tablespoons of turpentine
- ❑ 2 tablespoons of liquid detergent
- ❑ Small mixing bowl or cup
- ❑ Small piece of sponge
- ❑ Mirror

- ❑ Comic strip or cartoon from a newspaper (color or black-and-white)
- ❑ Blank piece of writing paper
- ❑ Spoon

What to Do

1. Mix the water, turpentine, and liquid detergent in the bowl.
2. Dab the liquid with the sponge, then onto the comic strip or cartoon you wish to copy.
3. Lay the writing paper on top of the cartoon.
4. Rub vigorously with the spoon until the image is clearly transferred to the writing paper.
5. Hold the cartoon up to a mirror.

 SAFETY NOTE: Use caution with turpentine, since it is a flammable substance.

Explanation

You were able to make a mirror copy of the cartoon, that is, the image is printed backwards. Turpentine and liquid detergent formed an emulsion capable of penetrating between the dye and oil particles of the dry printing ink, making the newsprint ink liquid again. Newsprint ink dissolves easily; however, note that glossy magazine paper contains too much lacquer and is not suitable for this activity.

THE CLEAN MACHINE

ACTIVITY-AT-A-GLANCE

Purpose

Explains how water goes through a filtration process.

When to Use

Curricular Area	Difficulty Level	Time to Do

Wastewater Treatment

2

15 minutes

What You'll Need

- ❏ 1-quart clay flowerpot with a hole at the bottom
- ❏ 2 coffee filters
- ❏ Pie pan or large wide-mouthed, clear plastic cup or beaker
- ❏ 1 cup each of crushed charcoal, sand, and gravel
- ❏ Water from a nearby lake, pond, or river
- ❏ 2 glass jars

What to Do

1. Line the clay pot with the coffee filters and set the pot in the pie pan.
2. Place a cup of each material in the filter-lined pot in the following order: charcoal, sand, and gravel, with the charcoal at the bottom.
3. Fill both glass jars with your water sample and observe. Notice the water's color or any foreign matter in the water.
4. Pour the water from one of the jars into the pot and allow the water to filter all the way through. This may take 5 to 10 minutes, depending on the size of your filtering materials and quality of your water.
5. Once the water is filtered, pour it from the pie pan back into the original jar.
6. Now compare the samples.

Explanation

Notice how much cleaner the filtered water is. This is a simple model of how a water-treatment filtration plant work. The large particles are trapped on top while the smaller particles are trapped near the bottom. Chemicals are added before and after the treatment process to kill many types of germs and bacteria. Consider a visit to a local wastewater treatment facility.

Variation

Try using different quantities of filtering materials.

WATERWORKS

 ACTIVITY-AT-A-GLANCE

Purpose

Demonstrates how heat affects water pressure.

When to Use

Curricular Area	Difficulty Level	Time to Do
Temperature; Water Pressure	**2**	 **5 minutes**

What You'll Need

- ❏ Plastic turkey baster
- ❏ Water
- ❏ Stove or other heating source
- ❏ Small pan
- ❏ Oven mitt or protective glove

What to Do

1. Suck up some of the cold water with the baster, and quickly turn the baster over. Observe. Then empty the baster.

2. Heat a small pan of water until the water is near the boiling point.

3. Wearing an oven mitt, suck up some of the hot water with the baster and quickly turn the baster over. (Do not squeeze the bulb of the baster.) Observe.

 SAFETY NOTE: Teacher activity only. Wear an oven mitt or protective glove to avoid being burnt by the hot water.

Explanation

When you turned over the baster of cold water, nothing happened. However, you observed the hot water shoot out of the turkey baster. This happened because when you heated the water, you also increased the water pressure. Warm air and water particles move faster than cold air and water particles; therefore, they exert a higher pressure. This pressure was strong enough to push the water out of the baster without your having to squeeze the bulb.

WATER, WATER, EVERYWHERE

ACTIVITY-AT-A-GLANCE

Purpose

Demonstrates how air and water pressure work.

When to Use

Curricular Area	Difficulty Level	Time to Do

Water and Air Pressure

5 minutes

(plus painting and drying time)

What You'll Need

- ❏ 2-liter plastic soda bottle
- ❏ One foot of $7/8$-inch (outside diameter) vinyl tubing
- ❏ Small nail
- ❏ Water
- ❏ Paint (any color)
- ❏ Medium-size paint brush
- ❏ Container (to catch the water)

What to Do

1. Place the vinyl tubing in the opening of the bottle, positioning it about $\frac{1}{2}$-inch from the bottom. (The fit will be very tight, but that is what you want.)

2. Cut off any excess tubing so that the tubing is level with the top of the bottle.

3. Paint the soda bottle so you cannot see the contents inside.

4. Using the nail, punch a small hole at the top of the bottle.

5. Fill the bottle with water.

6. Occasionally pour water out of the bottle into the empty container, but make sure you hold your finger over the hole whenever you pour out water.

7. Now, uncover the hole and observe that water will be forced up the tube when the bottle is set upright.

 SAFETY NOTE: Use caution when punching a hole in the bottle.

Explanation

This centuries-old apparatus is commonly known as a "Glorpy's Water of India" bottle. When the bottle is filled with water and the hole at the top of the bottle is left open, air pressure will force water up the tube. If the hole is covered and the bottle is inverted, only the water in the tube will come out. Set the bottle upright, with the hole left open, and the tube will refill. The purpose of painting the bottle is to allow observers to use their imagination as to what is happening in the bottle during the experiment.

Variation

Suggest that students make a drawing of what they hypothesize happens during this activity.

DON'T SPILL A DROP

 ### ACTIVITY-AT-A-GLANCE

Purpose

Illustrates the difference between surface tension and air pressure.

When to Use

Curricular Area	Difficulty Level	Time to Do

Water Pressure; Surface Tension

1

1 minute

What You'll Need

- ❏ 8-ounce drinking glass with a smooth rim (Do not use plastic.)
- ❏ Water
- ❏ Playing card, large enough to cover the rim or mouth of the glass

What to Do

1. Fill the glass to the top with water.
2. Place the card on top of the glass.
3. While holding the card, quickly invert the glass.
4. Remove your hand from the card. The water and card should remain in place, at least temporarily.

Explanation

Surface tension between the glass and water, and between the water and card, holds the card in place. Air pressure also helps this work. When the glass is inverted, a few drops of water leak out. This increases the volume of air inside the glass and decreases the air pressure inside the glass. The air pressure outside pushes the card against the mouth of the glass, holding it onto the water.

Variation

Fill the glass with different amounts of water and observe what happens. Try a different shape or size of glass and use different types of coverings.

BLACKLINES

Following are three forms that may be duplicated for classroom purposes:

1. A chart explaining Howard Gardner's theory of multiple intelligences and the skills students use in connection with those intelligences.

2. A reflection form for students to use as they observe or perform a scientific experiment/activity.

3. A performance assessment rubric designed for students and teachers to use for evaluation for a hands-on science course.

SkyLight Training and Publishing Inc.

GARDNER'S MULTIPLE INTELLIGENCES

Verbal/Linguistic Intelligence
The Intelligence of Words/Language
The ability to communicate through reading, writing, listening, or speaking.

Logical/Mathematical Intelligence
The Intelligence of Numbers and Reasoning
The ability to classify, predict, prioritize, formulate scientific hypotheses, and understand cause-effect relationships.

Visual/Spatial Intelligence
The Intelligence of Pictures and Images
The ability to see color, shape, form, spatial depth, and texture in the "mind's eye."

Bodily/Kinesthetic Intelligence
The Intelligence of the Whole Body and the Hands
The ability to control and interpret body motions, manipulate physical objects, and establish harmony between the mind and the body.

Musical/Rhythmic Intelligence
The Intelligence of Tone, Rhythm, and Timbre
The ability to respond emotionally to a pattern of sounds, create variations of musical patterns, and develop talent on musical instruments.

Interpersonal Intelligence
The Intelligence of Social Understanding
The ability to notice and distinguish moods, temperaments, motivations, and intentions; to understand and relate to others.

Intrapersonal Intelligence
The Intelligence of Self-Knowledge
The ability to know oneself and assume responsibility for one's life and learning.

Naturalist Intelligence
The Intelligence of Nature
The ability to recognize species as well as relationships in the environment and create taxonomies.

Adapted with permission from the Introduction to *Active Learning Handbook for the Multiple Intelligences Classroom* by James Bellanca, IRI/SkyLight Publishing.

STUDENT REFLECTION FORM

Observation is a very important part of the scientific inquiry method. For each hands-on science activity or experiment that is demonstrated or that you do on your own, answer the questions below.

Name of Science Activity /Experiment_____

WHAT did you observe?

HOW do you explain what you observed in this experiment?

HOW does what you learned in this science experiment connect to other things that you already know?

WHAT questions do you have about this experiment?

SCORING RUBRIC FOR THE SCIENCE COURSE

Using the following rating system, circle the number that best reflects student performance of the goals or objectives listed below.

Rating System: 1 = Poor   2 = Fair   3 = Good   4 = Excellent

Demonstrates understanding of scientific concepts.	1 2 3 4
Keeps accurate records of observations.	1 2 3 4
Organizes data/results through categorizing and ordering.	1 2 3 4
Draws logical conclusions from experimental results.	1 2 3 4
Effectively communicates scientific learning.	1 2 3 4
Transfers learning from one activity to another.	1 2 3 4
Relates prior knowledge to new learning.	1 2 3 4
Makes connections to science across the curriculum.	1 2 3 4
Makes inferences.	1 2 3 4
Applies knowledge to solve problems.	1 2 3 4
Uses lab equipment and supplies appropriately.	1 2 3 4
Demonstrates the scientific method.	1 2 3 4
Works cooperatively with others in lab situations.	1 2 3 4
Completes assignments on time.	1 2 3 4
Turns in work that is neatly done.	1 2 3 4

Teacher Comments:

GLOSSARY

Acid — A water-soluble sour compound.

Acid rain — Rain tainted with acids.

Adhesion — An attraction force that works when two different substances are brought in contact with one another.

Atom — The smallest part of an element that can combine with other atoms to form a molecule.

Base — A water-soluble bitter compound.

Bernoulli principle — The natural law that air pressure in a moving system is less than the pressure in the surrounding environment.

Casein — Milk protein.

Chemical bond — Electrical force that holds particles together.

Chemical reaction — A change that produces one or more new substances.

Chromatography — Extraction of solid material from a liquid.

Colloid — Material that has properties of both a liquid and a solid; a solution in which tiny undissolved particles are in suspension.

Crosslink — Material that strengthens the bonds between polymers.

Crystallize — The process by which particles of a liquid material re-form to make crystals as the liquid becomes solid.

Density — Measurement of mass of a certain volume of a material.

Electron — A negatively charged subatomic particle.

Evaporate — Changing from a liquid to a gas.

Freeze — Changing from a liquid to a solid.

Hydrocarbons — Chemical substances containing hydrogen and carbon.

Indicator — Chemical that changes color in acids and bases.

Inertia — The property of a substance or object that resists change when it is at rest or in motion.

Kinetic energy — Energy in moving objects.

Magnetism — Physical phenomena that include the attraction between iron and a magnet.

SkyLight Training and Publishing Inc.

Matter — Any substance or object that has mass and takes up space.

Molecules — Two or more atoms, chemically bonded, that make up all matter.

Neutralize — Process by which an acid and a base are mixed, with the resulting product being neither a base nor an acid.

Oxidation — The combination of oxygen with another material, such as iron. (Rust is called iron oxide.)

Polymer — A chemical compound; a chain formed by two or more molecules combining to form larger molecules containing structured units.

Potential energy — Stored energy.

Reflection — Light that has bounced off another object.

Saline — Containing salt, as in a saline solution.

Sublimation — Process by which a material changes from a solid directly to a gas.

Suspension — Mixture in which particles of a substance are temporarily suspended in a liquid.

Vacuum — Space where there is no matter; empty space.

Voltaic — Related to or producing an electrical current, as with a battery.

Volume — The amount of space occupied by an object or substance.

BIBLIOGRAPHY

Ardley, Neil. *The Science Book of Color.* San Diego: Harcourt, Brace, & Jovanovich, 1991.

———. *The Science Book of Electricity.* San Diego: Harcourt, Brace, & Jovanovich, 1991.

Barr, George. *Science Tricks and Magic for Young People.* New York, NY: Dover Publications, 1991.

Bellanca, James. *Active Learning Handbook for the Multiple Intelligences Classroom.* Arlington Heights, IL: IRI/SkyLight Publishing, 1997.

Berger, Sue, et al. *ChemPacs.* Batavia, IL: Flinn Scientific, 1989.

Breckenridge, Judy. *Simple Physics Experiments with Everyday Materials.* New York, NY: Sterling, 1993.

Brown, Robert J. *333 Science Tricks & Experiments.* Blue Ridge Summit, PA: McGraw, 1984.

———. *200 Illustrated Science Experiments for Children.* Blue Ridge Summit, PA: McGraw, 1987.

Catherall, Ed. *Exploring Light.* Austin, TX: Steck-Vaughn, 1990.

Churchill, Richard E. *Amazing Science Experiments with Everyday Materials.* New York, NY: Sterling, 1992.

Cobb, Vicki. *Science Experiments You Can Eat.* New York, NY: HarperCollins, 1994.

Devonshire, Hilary. *Color.* New York, NY: Franklin Watts, 1991.

Fitzpatrick, Julie. *Mirrors.* Morristown, NJ: Silver Burdett Press, 1984.

Gardner, Martin. *Entertaining Science Experiments with Everyday Objects.* New York, NY: Dover, 1981.

Gardner, Robert. *Science Projects about Electricity and Magnetism.* Hillside, NJ: Enslow, 1994.

Herbert, Don. *Mr. Wizard's Experiments for Young Scientists.* New York, NY: Doubleday, 1990

———. *Supermarket Science.* New York, NY: Random House, 1980.

Liem, Tik L. *Invitations to Science Inquiry.* 2d ed. Chino Hills, CA: Science Inquiry Enterprises, 1992.

Mandell, Muriel. *Simple Kitchen Experiments: Simple Science Experiments with Everyday Materials.* New York, NY: Sterling, 1993.

National Geographic Society. *Electricity and Simple Machines* (Videodisc).Washington, DC: National Geographic Society, 1995.

Parratore, Phil. *Chemistry.* Cypress, CA: Creative Teaching Press, 1995.

———. *Electricity & Magnetism.* Cypress, CA: Creative Teaching Press, 1995.

————. *Light & Sound.* Cypress, CA: Creative Teaching Press, 1995.

————. *Matter.* Cypress, CA: Creative Teaching Press, 1995.

————. *Wacky Science: A Cookbook for Elementary Teachers.* 2d ed. Dubuque, IA: Kendall/Hunt Publishing, 1998.

Sae, Andy. *Chemical Magic in the Grocery Store.* Portales, NM: Eastern New Mexico University, 1991.

Smithsonian Institution. *Color and Light: Step-by-Step Science Activity Projects from the Smithsonian Institution.* Milwaukee, WI: Gareth Stevens, 1993.

Van Cleave, Janice. *Chemistry for Every Kid: 101 Experiments That Really Work.* New York, NY: John Wiley & Sons, 1993.

————. *Magnets.* New York, NY: John Wiley & Sons, 1993.

————. *200 Gooey, Slippery, Slimy, Weird & Fun Experiments.* New York, NY: John Wiley & Sons, 1992.

Zubrowski, Bernie. *Blinkers and Buzzers: Building and Experimenting with Electricity.* New York, NY: William Morrow, 1991.

Index

A

Absorption of liquids, 138–39
Acetic acid, 5
Acid rain, effect of, on buildings, 4–5
Acids, 2–3
    chemical reactions with bases, 126–27, 136–37
    identification of, 136–37
Active learning, x
Adhesion, force of, 130–31
Agitation, 31
    as factor in dissolution of solution, 98–99
Air
    effect of temperature on volume of, 180–81
    movement of, 178–79
    space taken up by, 182–83
Air pressure
    changes in, 168–69
    demonstration showing, 190–91
    difference between surface tension and, 192–93
    and flexibility of polymers, 82–83
    and gas formation, 80–81
    and jet propulsion, 74–75, 170–71
    lack of, and gravity, 172–73
    power of, 38–39
    unequal, and movement of air, 178–79
Alcohol, flammability of, 16–17
Arches, and strength of eggshells, 36–37

B

Ball, effect of temperature on bounce of, 96–97
Bases, 2–3
    chemical reactions with acids, 126–27, 136–37
    identification of, 136–37
Battery
    demonstrating workings of, 48–49
    flow of electric current through homemade, 22–23
Block scheduling, deepening science experiences through, xi–xiii
Body oils and surface reactions, 26–27
Breath, demonstrating carbon dioxide in, 6–7, 58–59
Bubble gum, sugar in, 64–65
Bubbles
    in demonstrating chemical reactions, 2–3
    properties of, 76–77
    use of color to predicting popping of, 78–79
Buildings, effect of acid rain on, 4–5
Burning, as chemical process, 32–33
Butter, creation of, from cream, 30–31

C

Capillary action, 139
Carbon, 33, 47
Carbon dioxide, 3, 9, 25, 59, 81
    demonstrating presence of, in breath, 6–7, 57–58
Career education, xvi
Cartesian Diver, 176–77
Chemical breakdown of fruit juice, 46–47
Chemical changes
    decomposition as, 20–21
    demonstrating, 4–5
    and iron, 34–35
    and mothball density, 24–25
    and presence of carbon dioxide in breath, 6–7
Chemical indicators, 7
Chemical process, burning as, 32–33
Chemical properties of metals, 124–25
Chemical reactions
    between acids and bases, 126–27, 137–38
    creation of rust, 18–19
    demonstrating with household products, 2–3
    effect on temperature on, 106–7
    formation of gas during, 58–59
    in making polymer from food products, 44–45
    separation of milk into solid and liquid parts, 40–41
    stimulating volcanic eruptions with, 8–9
Chromatography, 138–39
Clouds, formation of, 162–63
Colloids, 41
Colors
    creation of, 118–19
    densities of, 120–21
    presence of, in sunlight, 128–29
    primary, 119
    secondary, 119
    visualization of, 132–33
Color spectrum, 129
Combustion, and flammability of alcohol, 16–17
Compaction, effect of pressure on, 50–51
Compass, making a, 146–47
Concave lens, 143
Condensation, 162–63
Conduction, demonstrating with batteries, 22–23, 48–49
Constants, xiii–xiv
Contraction of water, 100–101
Convex lens, 142–43
Cooling process, effect of evaporation on, 92–93

Copper, 49
Copper acetate, 125
Cream, creation of butter from, 30–31
Crystallization, 110–11, 134–35
    salt in, 12–13

D

Decomposition, oxygen as byproduct of, 20–21
Density
    of colors, 120–21
    and flammability of alcohol, 16–17
    and iceberg, 114–15
    of mothballs, 24–25
Dew, creation of, 94–95
Dew point, 95
Diffusion, 123
Dissolving, factors affecting, 98–99
Dry ice, characteristics of, 14–15

E

Earth formations and volcanic eruptions, 8–9
Eggshells, strength of, 36–37
Electric current, flow of, through homemade battery, 22–23
Electricity
    demonstrating with batteries, 48–49
    static, 148–49
        effects of, 150–51
        and the production of light, 164–65
        role of friction in causing, 152–53
Emulsion in copying newspaper prints, 184–85
Energy
    changes in, 42–43
    changing potential, to kinetic, 68–69
Epsom salts, 13
Evaporation, 134–35
    effect of, on cooling process, 92–93
Expansion of water, 100–101
Explosion, 91

F

Fat, as insulator against cold, 108–9
Field trips, xvi
Filtration of water, 186–87
Fingerprinting, 26–27
Flammability of alcohol, 16–17
Fluid pressure, nature of, 176–77
Flywheels, 61
Focal point, 145
Fog, creation of, 94–95

Food chemistry, composition of bubble gum, 64–65
Food products, making polymer from, 44–45
Foods, iron content of, 34–35
Force
    demonstrating with polymer, 72–73
    in overcoming friction, 62–63
    and power of air pressure, 38–39
Friction
    force in overcoming, 62–63
    role of, in causing static electricity, 152–53
Frostbite, 15
Fruit juice, chemical breakdown of, 46–47
Fungus. See Yeast

G

Gases
    formation of, during chemical reactions, 58–59
    properties of, 66–67
    thermal expansion of, 10–11
Gas formation
    and growth of yeast, 54–55
    in making polymer from food products, 44–45
    pressure in, 80–81
Glacier formation, demonstrating, 50–51
Glorpy's Water of India bottle, 191
Glucose, 65
Gravity
    center of, 84–85
    and lack of air pressure, 172–73
Guest speakers, xvi

H

Hands-on learning, x
Health. See also Human anatomy; Nutrition
    presence of carbon dioxide in breath, 6–7
Heat, intensification of, 88–89
Heat energy. See Temperature
Heat reactions, burning as, 32–33
Household products, demonstrating chemical reactions with, 2–3
Human anatomy
    body oils and surface reactions, 26–27
    and skin pores, 112–13

I

Icebergs, 114–15
Imposition, 91
Inertia, 60–61, 73
Insulators and temperature, 108–9
Intensification of heat, 88–89

Interference, effect of, on magnetic forces, 156–57
Iron content in food, 34–35
Iron deficiency, 35
Iron oxide, 19

J

Jet propulsion, 74–75, 170–71

K

Kinetic energy, changing potential energy to, 68–69

L

Lens
    concave, 143
    convex, 142–43
Light
    direction of, 154–55
    reflection of, 144–45, 154–55
        and creation of optical illusions, 158–59
    static electricity in production of, 164–65
Limestone, 5
Liquids, absorption of, 138–39

M

Magnesium sulfate, 13
Magnetic field, 147
Magnetic forces
    effect of interference on, 156–57
    passage of, through various materials, 160–61
Magnetism, and use of a compass, 146–47
Magnification, 142–43
Matter
    changes in, 42–43
    space occupied by, 52–53
Metal, chemical properties of, 124–25
Milk, separation into solid and liquid parts, 40–41
Mixtures/solutions
    creation of butter from cream, 30–31
    emulsion, 184–85
    factors in dissolution of, 98–99
    separation of milk, 40–41
Molecular movement, 52–53
    effect of temperature on, 70–71, 96–97, 98–99, 104–5
    and presence of colors in sunlight, 128–29
Mothballs
    density of, 24–25
    and sublimination, 102–3
Motion, 60–61
    and the need for force to overcome friction, 62–63

N

Newspaper prints, emulsion in copying, 184–85
Newton's First Law of Motion, 60–61, 62–63
    and polymer as powerful force, 72–73
Newton's Third Law of Motion, 72–73
    and jet propulsion, 74–75
Nutrition, iron content, 34–35

O

Optical illusions, 158–59
Optics, 88–89
    convex lens in, 142–43
    direction of light in, 154–55
    reflection of light, 144–45
    and visualization of color, 132–33
Osmosis, 123
Oxidation, and creation of rust, 18–19
Oxygen as byproduct of decomposition, 20–21

P

Particle size, as factor in dissolution of solution, 98–99
Performance assessment, xvi–xvii
Phase changes
    demonstrating, 102–3
        in dry ice, 14–15
    in energy and matter, 42–43
pH factor, 136–37
Physical changes
    in energy and matter, 42–43
    and popping of bubbles, 78–79
    salt crystallization, 12–13
Physical properties, demonstrating, 76–77
Physics, and strength of eggshells, 36–37
Plant nourishment, 122–23
Polymers
    and composition of bubble gum, 64–65
    flexibility of, 82–83
    interaction of molecules in, 70–71
    making, from food products, 44–45
    as powerful force, 72–73
Potential energy, changing, to kinetic energy, 68–69
Pressure, effect of, on compaction, 50–51
Primary colors, 119
Properties of air, 182–83

R

Rainbow, 129
Reflection of light, 144–45, 154–55
    and creation of optical illusions, 158–59

SkyLight
Training and Publishing Inc.

We Prepare Your Teachers Today for the Classrooms of Tomorrow

Learn from Our Books and from Our Authors!

Ignite Learning in Your School or District.

SkyLight's team of classroom-experienced consultants can help you foster systemic change for increased student achievement.

Professional development is a process, not an event. SkyLight's seasoned practitioners drive the creation of our on-site professional development programs, graduate courses, research-based publications, interactive video courses, teacher-friendly training materials, and online resources—call SkyLight Training and Publishing, Inc. today.

SkyLight specializes in three professional development areas.

Specialty # **Best Practices**

We **model** the best practices that result in improved student performance and guided applications.

Specialty # **Making the Innovations Last**

We help set up **support** systems that make innovations part of everyday practice in the long-term systemic improvement of your school or district.

Specialty # **How to Assess the Results**

We prepare your school leaders to encourage and **assess** teacher growth, **measure** student achievement, and **evaluate** program success.

Contact the SkyLight team and begin a process toward long-term results.

SkyLight
Training and Publishing Inc.

2626 S. Clearbrook Dr., Arlington Heights, IL 60005
800-348-4474 • 847-290-6600 • FAX 847-290-6609

There are
one-story intellects,
two-story intellects, and three-story
intellects with skylights. All fact collectors, who
have no aim beyond their facts, are one-story men. Two-story men
compare, reason, generalize, using the labors of the fact collectors as
well as their own. Three-story men idealize, imagine,
predict—their best illumination comes from
above, through the skylight.
—*Oliver Wendell*
Holmes

Training and Publishing Inc.